Modernity, Ethnicity and Development

Modernity, Ethnicity and Development

D. V. Kumar

RAWAT PUBLICATIONS
Jaipur • New Delhi • Bangalore • Guwahati • Kolkata

ISBN 978-81-316-0846-3

Published by
Prem Rawat for **Rawat Publications**
Satyam Apts, Sector 3, Jawahar Nagar, Jaipur 302 004 (India)
Phone: 0141 265 1748 / 7006 Fax: 0141 265 1748
E-mail: info@rawatbooks.com
Website: www.rawatbooks.com

New Delhi Office
4858/24, Ansari Road, Daryaganj, New Delhi 110 002
Phone: 011 2326 3290

Also at *Bangalore*, *Guwahati* and *Kolkata*

Typeset by Rawat Computers, Jaipur
Printed at Chaman Enterprises, New Delhi

Contents

Preface

I have been interested in the study of modernity and its critical relationship with ethnicity for quite some time now. I have tried to share my thoughts about this with interested readers in terms of articles in journals and edited books. It began to dawn on me that it would be a good idea to bring them together at one place so that what I have tried to articulate at different times and places would be available at one place. I have been quite encouraged by the feedback to this idea I have received from some of my friends and colleagues.

Modernity has emerged as a metanarrative in social science literature. Although it has been used quite frequently, its deeper meaning and the different forms of engagement it entails have not been adequately dealt with. Also, it has been uncritically accepted that Europe was the only home of modernity without realizing that other civilizations also contributed significantly to the project of modernity, a point which I have tried to emphasize in the second chapter. Furthermore, the classical scholarship (writings of Marx, Durkheim and Weber) reflected on the relationship between modernity and ethnicity and came to the conclusion that ethnic identities would diminish in the context of modernity and development. However, social reality is too complex to be captured in such a simplistic formulation as it can be clearly seen that ethnic and nationalist aspirations have indeed become stronger than ever before. In fact, some would argue that it is modernity itself with its hegemonic and homogenizing logic that leads to the strengthening of these identities. I have tried to look at some of these issues both at theoretical and empirical levels. Tribal development, especially in the context of the North-East, has also been an area of my interest. While looking at the issue of development in the North-East, there is a strong need to be sensitive to the aspirations and resource base of the area. Any plans and programmes that do not take into account the sensitivities and sensibilities of the people of the region are bound to fail as successive governments have realized. One of the chapters deals with this issue as tribal development is an organic and inseparable part of the larger issue of modernity that is sought to be implanted in the North-Eastern region.

Acknowledgements

The present volume is a collection of my articles that have appeared in different journals and edited books over a period of time. I am extremely thankful to the editors and publishers for permitting me to reproduce the articles in this volume. Chapter 1 appeared in *Sociological Bulletin* (2008). Chapters 2, 3 and 6 appeared in the *Eastern Anthropologist* (in 2013, 2006 and 2011, respectively). Chapter 4 appeared in my edited volume on *Modernity and Ethnic Processes in India* (2014). The chapter on 'Gellnerian Theory of Nation and Nationalism' appeared in *Sociological Bulletin* (2010). Chapter 7 appeared in an edited volume (2014) by Ishwar Modi. Chapter 8 was first published in an edited volume on *Peace and Development in Mizoram* (2007). Chapter 9 on 'Tribal Development' appeared in the *Encyclopaedia of Social Work in India,* which was edited by Surendra Singh. Chapter 10 was first published in an edited volume on *Tribal Communities and the Exclusion-Inclusion Debate in India* (2010) by Ganesha Somayaji. The last chapter on 'State and Civil Society' appeared in an edited volume on *Civil Society, Voluntary Sector and Social Transformation in India* (2014).

I am also thankful to T. K. Oommen, Prasenjit Biswas and others who encouraged me to bring together these articles as they would be of interest to the students and scholars who are engaged in a critical study of modernity, ethnicity and development.

I would also like to thank Rawat Publications, especially Pranit Rawat, for showing interest in the publication of this volume.

Last but not the least, I would like to thanks my children Lahari and Pranay, who have been keenly enquiring about this volume.

1

Engaging with modernity

Need for a critical negotiation

Modernity has had a deeply critical impact on the social structures and cultural institutions across the globe. Its influence spread through every nook and corner of the world. Modernity when it embarked upon its journey of reaching everywhere did have tremendous political and intellectual backing. Famed philosophers such as Voltaire, Hume, Rousseau, Kant, Adam Smith and others were deeply supportive of the Enlightenment Project (in the eighteenth-century Europe) that actually led to the consolidation of modernity. Later on, colonialism became a vehicle through which modernity made an inexorable entry into every possible society. Without such solid political and intellectual backing, it would not have spread the way it did. In terms of reach and intensity, there were few phenomena that achieved the breadth and scale of the support that modernity achieved in its wake. There is hardly any society that has remained immune to the influence of modernity, and the degree to which it has influenced different societies is quite profound. Modernity, therefore, does demand serious and sustained engagement from us.

Though modernity is said to have begun in the West in about the fifteenth century (a notion that has been contested; the next chapter focuses in depth on this issue), it acquired its distinctive character in the context of the Enlightenment Project in the eighteenth century (Pathak 1998, p. 17). By the term 'Project' one might get the impression that there was an absolutely coherent and unchallenged set of ideas present in the Project and that there was complete agreement among philosophers who worked within its framework. This is not our position. There were different voices within the Project that demanded their own space and supremacy. However, what is undeniable about the Project is that it did contain a set of distinctive underlying assumptions and expectations that were to guide social life in the years to come. Some of these assumptions and expectations such as reason, science, progress, empiricism and secularism, as and when they were realized, were supposed to contribute significantly to the enhancement of human condition.

Although modernity has emerged as one of the most powerful and 'hegemonic' categories, the nuances and implications the term 'modernity' evokes still remain deeply contested. How do we look at modernity? How do we engage ourselves with it? What are the tensions and challenges that one may experience trying to engage with modernity in different ways? These are some of the principal questions that this chapter will attempt to explore in detail.

Different ways of looking at modernity

There are three ways, which are different if not contradictory to one another, in which one can possibly look at modernity: (i) as a *philosophical idea*, (ii) as a *form of society* and (iii) as an *experience* (Callinicos 1999, p. 297). As an *idea*, it represents a radical rupture with the past and thus privileges progress, science, optimism and universality and critiques superstitions, blind faiths and pessimism. It encourages us to adopt alternative ways of looking at the world and its possibilities. Whereas in the past the idea of God reigned supreme; however, with the emergence of modernity the idea of reason became dominant. Through the instrument of reason, it is possible to understand and explain the world. Invariable laws of nature, it was contended, are possible to formulate. Reason thus became the dominant mode of discourse. Modernity was conceived as the celebration of objective and instrumental reason (Kumar 2006, p. 2). It struck at the very structure of tyrannical practices and superstitions. Immanuel Kant, a celebrated advocate of modernity and its institutions, said, 'Do not wrest from reason that which makes it the highest good on earth, i.e. the prerogative of being the ultimate touchstone of truth' (Kant 1788/1949, p. 305). It no longer looks to the past for its legitimacy and justification. It looks to the future and creates its own self-justification. As Habermas argued, 'Modernity can and will no longer borrow the criterion by which it takes its orientation from the models supplied by another epoch: it has to create its own normativity out of itself' (Habermas 1987, p. 7). The idea of modernity is irretrievably linked to the idea of progress and science. Modernity views progress as inevitable and that human advancement will continue unabated. Hunger, ignorance and superstition that dominated the larger society in the past will slowly but surely disappear. Such was the unbounded optimism with which the idea of modernity came into being.

Second, modernity can also be looked at as a form of society that would be characterized by distinctive economic, political and social characteristics. Economically, there would be increasing mechanization of production (use of inanimate sources of energy; Levy 1966), a shift from agriculture to industry, growth of urbanization as workers move from place to place where industries are located, growth of cash economy, consolidation of free market economy, monopoly capitalism and so on. Politically there would be increasing decentralization, democratization, greater participation of people in the decision-making process, growth of bureaucracy and welfare policies due to public pressure. In the social sphere, a modern society has come to be associated with important shifts in values and institutional devices. In terms of value-orientations, as Parsons argued, there would be a shift from particularism to universalism, ascription to achievement, functional diffuseness to functional specificity and, finally, collective orientation to self-orientation (1964, pp. 339–357). The former are characteristic of traditional societies and the latter of modern societies; for example,

Parsons regarded the Australian aboriginal society as primitive, characterized as it was by its value orientations such as collective-orientation, ascription and so on, and at the other end of the evolutionary scale are advanced civilizations such as Western Europe, the USA and the erstwhile Soviet Union, which are considered modern given their dominant value orientations such as self-orientation, achievement and so on. However, it needs to be pointed out here that Parsons did not regard modern society as one that is completely and exclusively characterized by its value orientations such as universalism, achievement, functional specificity and self-orientation. Nevertheless, those value orientations are certainly more dominant in those advanced societies. In terms of institutional devices, Parsons says that market, money and bureaucracy were the most important institutional universals found in a modern society. Structural differentiation and functional specialization are but a pervasive feature of any modern society.

Third, modernity can also be looked at as an experience, an experience that is full of contradictions. On one hand, it promises many things, including progress, advancement, removal of ignorance, power and joy for its members. On the other hand, it seeks to destroy everything, including our core values that characterize our empathy and respect for collective welfare as humans, for it introduces an element of uncertainty, risk and confusion by celebrating competition, open market and allowing the jungle doctrine of survival-of-the-fittest to dominate the collective psyche. Marshall Berman had put it quite succinctly. One cannot help but quote him at length:

> There is a mode of vital experience – experience of space and time, of the self and others, of life's possibilities and perils – that is shared by men and women all over the world today. I will call this body of experience 'modernity'. To be modern is to find ourselves in an environment that promises us adventure, power, joy, growth, transformation of ourselves and the world – and, at the same time, that threatens to destroy everything we have, everything we know and everything we are. Modern environments and experiences cut across all boundaries of geography and ethnicity, of class and nationality, of religion and ideology: in this sense modernity can be said to unite all mankind. But it is a paradoxical unity, a unity of

> disunity: it pushes us into a maelstrom of perpetual disintegration and renewal, of struggle and contradiction, of ambiguity and anguish. To be modern is to be part of a universe in which, as Marx said, 'all that is solid melts into air'. (1982, p. 15)

Thus, as one can see, there are different, if not contradictory to one another, ways of looking at modernity. Each way of looking at modernity would make us sensitive to each aspect of modernity. The first one would highlight the philosophical aspects of modernity. The second one would enable us to look at the empirical manifestations of modernity. The third one would provide us with a profound account of the psychosocial aspects of modernity. There has been rich sociological literature on such aspects published by Indian scholars.[1]

Forms of engagement

As stated at the outset, what is compelling about modernity is that it has the power to demand, and succeeds in extracting, serious engagement from us. One cannot remain immune to the deeply consequential aspects of modernity. What are the different forms in which we engage ourselves with modernity? Broadly one can identify three forms. They are (i) celebration and eulogization of modernity, (ii) negation and rejection of modernity (either in its present form or complete rejection of the very epistemology on which it is based), and (iii) critical and creative negotiation with modernity. The second form of engagement, that is, rejection of modernity, may be misunderstood and wrongly held that it is no form of engagement at all. It is our considered view that that the very act of rejection presupposes certain kind of engagement, though in a negative way.

Celebration of modernity

One way of engaging with modernity is to celebrate it. This involves eulogizing it, looking at it as a great possibility. Exploration of this possibility and its concretization may completely change the way we live and the way we look at the world. With modernity life will increasingly become orderly and free from the kind of problems that characterize the world. Poverty, superstition and blind beliefs will give way to knowledge, prosperity and rational outlook. Control over nature, which can be used as a tremendous resource, will enhance our standard of life and lead to general prosperity. By privileging reason, it would increasingly become possible for us to understand and explain the world through invariable laws of nature. Modernity will do away with the constraints imposed by tradition, customs, beliefs and feelings. Reason will sweep away social and political beliefs and forms of organization that are not based on scientific proofs. Life will no longer be ruled by the notion of God or divine power. It is no longer necessary to submit to the will of a Supreme Being. Such a celebratory tone can be noticed in the writings of philosophers of Enlightenment; for example, Rousseau who remained a steadfast supporter of modernity and its emancipatory potential because of its privileging of rationality was constantly driven by a desire to struggle against the obstacles that obscure knowledge and communication (cited in Touraine 1995, p. 17). To resolve conflicts among individuals, social contract comes into being. Social contract is nothing but the embodiment of reason. He does not see divine revelation as the organizing principle behind society and replaces it with reason. The education of an individual must be such that it must free him from the narrow and irrational vision forced upon him by his family and his own passion. It must expose him to rational knowledge and prepare him to be part of a society that emphasizes reason. It must enable him to organize his life on the basis of rational principles that are constantly stressed upon by the discourse of modernity. The philosophical thought of Kant and Hegel too can be characterized as the celebration of reason and modernity (Habermas 1987, Touraine 1995). More recently, the modernization theory propounded since 1950s and 1960s is nothing but an undiluted acceptance of modernity and its institutions (Black 1966, Hoselitz 1960, Lerner 1958, Levy 1966, Moore 1967, Parsons 1964, Smelser 1969, Stephenson 1968). Historically, up until post-Second-World-War period, very little interest was shown in the changes occurring in different societies (Pandey 1988, p. 7). The study of social changes assumed great significance in the 1950s and 1960s when new nations came into existence and the colonial empire gradually faded. Interest began to be shown on the nations as to how they intended to fulfil the massive expectations of their peoples and with what institutional devices. Funds began to be allocated generously for conducting studies.

Modernization became the main instrument through which massive changes can be initiated. It was held that problems of poverty, disease, ignorance and poor infrastructural facilities can only be removed by undertaking the process of modernization initiated in the West. Although it was viewed by some as a hegemonic device employed by the West to push through its own agenda of neocolonialism, it was celebrated as the panacea for all the evils that plagued the Third World societies, such as Asia, Africa and Latin America. Modernization theories propounded in the 1950s and 1960s reflected the dominant mood during that time, which was that of privileging modernization and the massive changes that accompanied it.

Persistent perusal of the process of modernization will enable the 'underdeveloped' societies to reach the level of prosperity that is currently seen in the West. It is only in the interests of these societies that they adopt the value orientations, institutional devices and structural aspects that are present in advanced and industrial societies. What had added impetus to this was the process of globalization that had entrenched itself. Globalization is but a logical extension of modernity. It only seeks to advance further the ideas of reason, progress, universality and optimism. Among the people mentioned above, there are not many who would like to problematize the very idea of modernity itself and engage with the pathological forms it *assumes when left to itself.*

Negation/rejection of modernity

The second form of engagement pursued is negating modernity and its institutions. There have been extremely powerful voices that positioned themselves in opposition to modernity and whatever it stood for. Such voices can be broadly divided into Critical Theory and Postmodern Theory. The Critical Theory emerged out of the collective efforts of all those associated with what came to be known as the Frankfurt School (established in the 1920s in Germany). Although there were differences among the theorists on several issues, what had kept them united was a desire to critically engage with the issues of the day. One of them certainly was modernity and its pathological dimensions. They launched an extremely powerful and scathing critique of modernity. Modernity led to the growth of technological rationality (instrumental rationality), consumer culture, commodification and instrumentalization of social relations and abstract and impersonal relations. Reason instead of becoming an instrument of liberation and emancipation has in fact become an instrument of oppression and hegemony. The tendency to homogenize and degrade diversities is an offshoot of modern sensibilities. From Adorno to Horkheimer to Marcuse we see the growing disenchantment with modernity. The two world wars, emergence of fascist regimes, sharpening of socioeconomic inequalities, the continuous ecological destruction are all outcomes of a project that has scant regard for human lives and cultural sensibilities guided as it is by dehumanizing and hegemonizing technological rationality. There is a certain degree of erosion of criticality and creativity leading to a pronounced inability to deal with issues of exploitation, oppression and discrimination; for example, Herbert Marcuse, one of the best known theorists of the Frankfurt School, if he were discussing about an important outcome of modernity, that is, consumer culture, may argue that the growth of consumer culture has clearly dented revolutionary potential and social critique. People are seduced by commodities and comfort. They are content in their material affluence and happy to wallow in the false freedoms provided by leisure and sexual opportunities. He said that subjectivities had been shaped by the needs of the capitalistic system. The one-dimensional man is a shallow person living an illusory life, voluntarily seeking to fulfil false needs. He wrote, 'Most of the prevailing needs to relax, have fun, to behave and consume in accordance with the advertisements, to love and hate what others love and hate, belong to this category of false needs' (1972, p. 19).

Needless to repeat, the growing consumer culture engendered by capitalist modernization has a lot to do with this. Marcuse became extremely popular among students across different university campuses for his call for an authentic and non-repressive sexuality as a perfect antidote to alienation under capitalist modernization.

While critical theorists based their critique of modernity on the pathological form it has assumed – its excessive use of technological rationality, growth of commodification and instrumentalization of social relations and consumer culture and so on – postmodernists rejected the very *epistemology* on which it is based. The essential components of the epistemology of modernity are science, objectivity, certainty, progress and truth. Postmodernists' engagement with modernity is based on their rejection of the following Enlightenment tenets (McLennan 1992, p. 330):

- Our knowledge of society, like society itself, is holistic, cumulative and broadly progressive in character.
- We can attain rational knowledge of society.
- Such knowledge is universal and thus objective.
- Sociological knowledge is both different from, and superior to, distorted forms of thought, such as ideology, religion, common sense, superstition and prejudice.
- Social scientific knowledge, once validated and acted upon, can lead to mental liberation and social betterment among humanity generally.

A closer look at the above tenets may tell us that the Enlightenment Project seeks to attain an 'objective' and 'impartial' knowledge, which is called science and is viewed as superior to what are called 'narratives', which are essentially stories or fables invented to give meaning and significance to our lives. The epistemology on which modernity is based takes the position that stories or tales do not provide real or true knowledge and their main function is to provide only existential or ideological comforts to us as we go through life. Stories and fables do not enable us to acquire objective, scientific and universal knowledge about the social reality. Their relevance is limited to local, personal and social contexts. In fact, they have the status of *myths*.

One can find a lucid rejection of the above in Lyotard's *The Postmodern Condition* (1984). He reacts sharply to such an understanding of Enlightenment by saying that its view of pure and true knowledge is itself a *grand myth.* One cannot possibly come across a more powerful and hegemonic myth than that of scientific or objective knowledge. Scientific and objective knowledge is justified in the name of progress and emancipation, which are, as he would argue, metanarratives. One may not give much credence to such narratives after one has seen events like world wars, ecological destruction, growing inequalities and frustration among youth, issues that perpetually beleaguer human society.

The very ideas of certainty, objectivity, truth, history, optimism and progress that modernity tried to privilege have been subjected to a scathing critique. It is argued that we should adopt 'incredulity towards metanarratives', thus privileging uncertainty, fragmentation, subjectivity, difference, relativism and pessimism. Knowledge, which is considered the exclusive preserve of philosophers, scholars and scientists, needs to be taken out of their hold and subjected to a deconstructive reading and, thus, in the process, destroying the hegemonic construction of knowledge itself.

Critical and creative negotiation with modernity

The third way of engaging with modernity is to negotiate with it in a critical and self-reflexive way. Here the idea is not to eulogize or reject it in an unproblematical way; one must not only look at the possibilities and opportunities it affords but also examine the pathologies, paradoxes, ambiguities and contradictions that constitute modernity. This kind of engagement starts with the premise that modernity does have enormous potential in changing the course of human history and the way we imagine the world and actualize it. One thing that is indisputable about modernity is that it has made human life completely different from what it was before characterized as it was by helpless submission to divine power. There was an implicit acceptance of an inability to do anything about the world (on one's own) that was full of ignorance, superstitions and blind faith. One had no choice but to succumb to the vagaries of nature. It would behave the way the divine power ordered it to do. Modernity has changed that. It has given us the power not only to understand the world and the way we live but also to change it in a way to benefit and enhance our collective well-being. At the same time, however, it has acquired certain pathologies. For one it has become hegemonic. The only way of understanding the world, it is repeated ad infinitum, is through the instrument of reason. All other ways of looking and understanding societies, cultures, processes and institutions are denigrated. Reason has become an instrument of oppression. Feelings, faith and folk tales as the alternative ways of understanding the world were thoroughly undermined. Apart from the above, it has led to certain other pathological tendencies that need to be understood and grappled with. Otherwise what is a great possibility will be turned into an unmitigated disaster. Nuclear wars, ecological destruction in the name of development, sharpening of socioeconomic inequalities, growing sense of alienation and anomie are some of the starkly visible fallouts of modernity that have troubled the minds of outstanding thinkers.

Such a critical appreciation of modernity could be noticed in the writings of celebrated sociologists such as Marx, Durkheim and Weber and more recently in those of Habermas, Giddens and Touraine. Although Marx, Durkheim and Weber broadly contributed within the framework of Enlightenment and of modernity and are deeply appreciative of the 'functional' aspects of modernity and its institutions, they did not hesitate to put forward a powerful critique of modernity. They eulogized and critiqued almost in the same breath; for example, as Marshall Berman (1982) said, the Communist Manifesto can also be read as the Modern Manifesto. Terms like 'modern industry', 'modern worker', 'modern state power', 'modern productive forces', appear many times. It may be argued that the Communist Manifesto is the first major sociopolitical affirmation of modernity. Marx was deeply conscious of liberating and modernizing the potential of science. It would lead to the development of productive forces. At the same time, he spoke of alienation – a pathological socioeconomic condition in which workers feel alienated from themselves, from others, from products and finally from the productive process itself. Capitalism (which can be viewed as an offshoot of modernity) and private property distort human relations, deprive man of his creativity, the joy in his work and cripple his relationship with nature, women, community and the larger world (quoted in Pathak 1998, p. 21). He provided a scathing critique of capitalist institutions and their functions.

Emile Durkheim (1964) noted the historical significance of transition from societies characterized by mechanical solidarity to those characterized by organic solidarity. In the former, solidarity is based on likeness. People differ least in terms of their values, likes, dislikes, attitudes and so on. Collective conscience embraces greater part of individual consciousness. People are not free to pursue their own interests. The hold of collective conscience, however, begins to weaken when societies move towards a state of organic solidarity that is caused by an increase in volume and material density of society. Individual consciousness begins to flourish, which itself is a greater emancipatory and liberating development. Although Durkheim was appreciative of the liberating potential of modernity, he articulated his sense of discomfort and unease with what such potential can produce, that is, anomie. Anomie is not a state of normlessness, as it is popularly misunderstood. It is a state where conformity to norms is considerably weakened because of rapid economic and social changes that mark a developing or developed society. There is a breakdown of moral order, a negative aspect of modernity. Thus, Durkheim calls for strengthening of moral community so that societies do not break down because of the unstoppable march of modernity. Max Weber too spoke of the great potential of rationalization (an essential modern attribute) and its institutionalization through bureaucracy and at same time referred to the growing disenchantment of people. There is a loss of meaning caused by the process of disenchantment, which itself is a product of modernity.

Giddens, one of the most celebrated and influential thinkers on modernity and its institutions, is severely critical of postmodernist thinkers and their rejection of whatever modernity stands for: its certainty, optimism, progress and idea of history (1990, pp. 46–53). He rejects the idea that no systematic knowledge of human beings or trends of social development is possible. If it were so, even postmodernists could not have written whatever they wrote. What postmodernists are talking about today, Nietzsche dwelt upon it a century ago when something called postmodern sensibilities did not exist, which only goes to show that the critique of modernity was part of modernity itself and its capacity to deal with multiple and conflicting perspectives. It is part of the growing radicalization of modernity that postmodernists are talking about. The critique of certainty is inherent in modernity itself. There is no such thing as knowledge in conditions of high modernity. Knowledge becomes hypothesis.

Modernity is regarded as consisting of those institutions and modes of behaviour that first appeared in post-feudal Europe but have increasingly become world-historical in impact. The central institutional features encompassing modernity are industrialism (social relations implied in the widespread use of material power and machinery in production processes), capitalism (a system of commodity production), surveillance (supervisory control of subject populations) and nation-state. The institutions mentioned above and which are associated with modernity are qualitatively different from those that existed before them in the sense that they are essentially reflexive and dynamic entities. The pace of change is much faster. The scope of change is wider. As Giddens (1991) argued, the profoundness with which it affects pre-existing social practices and modes of behaviour is much greater.

As stated earlier, modernity here is conceived of as a highly dynamic system. What lends dynamism to modernity are three essential elements. They are (i) separation of time and space, (ii) disembedding of social relations and (iii) reflexivity. What is distinctive about pre-modern cultures is that they had their own method of reckoning of time, and time and space were necessarily connected through the situatedness of place. The separation of time and space in a modern setting provides a basis for the recombination of social relations with reference to the particularity of time, which is essential for the modern-day organizations to exist.

Modern social organizations presume the precise coordination of the actions of many human beings physically absent from one another (Giddens 1991, p. 18). The second element of disembedding of social relations refers to the 'lifting-out' of social relations from local contexts and their rearticulation across indefinite tracts of the time–space continuum (p. 18). This is the key to the tremendous acceleration in time–space distanciation that is introduced by modernity. The third element that modernity is associated with is reflexivity, which is the susceptibility of most aspects of social activities and material relations with nature, to chronic revision in light of new information and knowledge (p. 18). Reflexivity is an integral part of social sciences, and social sciences do not simply accumulate knowledge as natural sciences do.

Yet Giddens is acutely aware of some of the challenges associated with modernity. A modern society is essentially a risk society. In view of the gradual weakening of traditional sources of support, the element of risk becomes that much greater. Under conditions of modernity, the future is continually drawn into the present by means of the reflexive organization of knowledge environment (Giddens 1991, p. 3). Rise of new risks unknown in the past is a real danger. Coupled with the element of risk is the element of personal meaninglessness, a feeling that life has nothing much to contribute, which in turn becomes a psychological problem seen afflicting people in the context of late modernity. Giddens is also opposed to all kinds of 'foundationalism' promoted in the name of modernity. This refers to the belief that it is possible to acquire certain knowledge about the society that is beyond all kinds of doubts and questions. Modernity in the true sense of the term would not approve of such optimism, as reflexivity and self-doubt are an organic part of modernity itself. There is a need to deepen such reflexivity that will lead to a heightened process of radicalization of modernity. Modernity should be capable of coming to terms with its own reflexivity (Pathak 1998, p. 29).

There are equally powerful voices that are not only appreciative of the liberating potential of modernity but also express a sense of discomfiture with certain pathological forms it has assumed. One such voice is that of Habermas (1985, 1987). Coming to the defence of modernity against the critique of Enlightenment by postmodernity, Habermas asserts that modernity has a great emancipatory and conscience-raising role to play. Modernity could not achieve what it wanted to achieve because its potential has not been realized sufficiently. That is why Habermas speaks in terms of the unfinished project of modernity. The need is to understand and realize its massive potential. However, there lies a challenge in encountering modernity. The challenge is to fight the technological rationality that has come to be associated with modernity. Modernity has been reduced to nothing more than instrumental rationality. Technological rationality is devoid of core human values such as equality, democracy and human solidarity. It leads to bureaucratization and commodification. It leads to a loss of meaning and sense of society being uprooted from, and divested of, such values that give sustenance to human life. Therefore, the conundrum that we need to resolve given the inflexible nature of technological rationality, especially when used as a guide post to conduct the society's affairs within the confines of modernity, is how to rescue modernity from its obsession with instrumental/technological rationality and strive for a fuller realization of its emancipatory potential. This is where Habermas's theory of communicative rationality becomes pertinent (1984). This consists of the undistorted activities of people genuinely attempting to attain a clear mutual understanding. It is only by engaging in an authentic, dialogical and reciprocal communication that modernity can ensure joy, happiness, emancipation and freedom. Poststructuralist thinkers such as Foucault would, however, question whether the Enlightenment project can or indeed should be salvaged at all. Others have pointed to the utopian aspects of his theory. Foucault, for example, talks about authentic and dialogical communication without referring to the institutional forms such as diverse media and grass-roots social movements required to support such a system of communication.

Talking about such institutional forms, Touraine refers to one of such forms – the terrain of social movement. Social movement is the terrain where one can bring 'reason' and 'subject' together. He subjected modernity to a scathing critique without abandoning the relevance of or need for the realization of the efficacy of instrumental reason or the liberating power of critical thought and individualism. His main argument is that modernity introduced a dualism between reason and subject, and rationalization and subjectivation, privileging the former over the latter. Reason has begun to be reified and thus put on a pedestal. Subject has been relegated to the background. Foucault attempts to introduce a dialogue between the two. To quote him, 'Without Reason, the Subject is trapped into an obsession with identity: Without the Subject, Reason becomes an instrument of might. In this century, we have seen both the dictatorship of Reason and totalitarian perversion of the subject. . . . Is it not possible that they begin to speak to each other and to learn to live together?' (Touraine 1995, p. 6). Touraine attempts to extricate modernity from a historical tradition that has reduced it to rationalization and to introduce the theme of the personal subject and subjectivation (p. 6). He speaks of a compelling need to bring reason and subject together, and possibly the agent of such a union is the social movement or, in other words, the transformation of the personal and collective defence of the subject into a collective action directed against power, which subordinates reason to its own interests (p. 374).

Conclusion

As one can see, the most meaningful form of engagement with modernity would be a critical and creative engagement. Uncritical and blind celebration of modernity, as modernization theories of the 1960s and 1970s tended to do, will not enable us to appreciate the problems, paradoxes and tensions associated with modernity. Its excessive stress or in fact reification of reason, technological rationality, commodification and instrumentalization of social relations; its tendency to homogenize; and its discrediting of the 'local', 'personal' and 'myths' needs to be critiqued. In addition, the total pessimism exhibited by some of the critical theorists and almost all the postmodernists while engaging with modernity is highly problematical. Despite the pathological forms it assumes, modernity if not *handled properly* will speak a different language, a language that is full of optimism and liberating potential. It was modernity that liberated us from the tyranny of tradition and superstition and tried to create a dialogic space. It enhanced and deepened the sphere of reflexivity, as Giddens would argue.

Thus, it is not only important to be conscious of modernity's potential as a pragmatic and powerful change agent and its reflexivity but also remain alert and sensitive to the possibility of its changing into a hegemonic, dehumanizing and homogenizing Orwellian doctrine that subsists on technological rationality. Therefore, a critical and creative engagement is precisely the kind of engagement that we should be using to engage with modernity

NOTE

1. Some important writings on modernity/modernization include the following: Yogendra Singh's *Modernisation of Indian Tradition* (1973), Ashis Nandy's *The Intimate Enemy: Loss and Recovery of Self under Colonialism* (1994), Dipankar Gupta's *Mistaken Modernity: India between Worlds* (2000) and, more recently, Avijit Pathak's *Modernity, Globalisation and Identity: Towards a Reflexive Quest* (2006). A detailed discussion of such rich literature is beyond the scope of this work and thus such a pursuit may have to be undertaken in a future work.

REFERENCES

Berman, M. 1982. *All That Is Solid Melts into Air: The Experience of Modernity*. London: Verso.

Black, C. E. 1966. *The Dynamics of Modernization: A Study in Comparative History*. New York: Harper and Row.

Callinicos, A. 1999. *Social Theory: A Historical Introduction*. Cambridge, UK: Polity.

Durkheim, E. 1964. *The Division of Labor in Society*. New York: Free Press.

Giddens, A. 1990. *The Consequences of Modernity*. Cambridge, UK: Polity.

———. 1991. *Modernity and Self-identity: Self and Society in the Late Modern Age*. Cambridge, UK: Polity.

Habermas, J. 1984. *The Theory of Communicative Action*. Boston, MA: Beacon.

———. 1985. Modernity: An incomplete project. In H. Foster (ed.), *Postmodern Culture* (pp. 78–101). Cambridge, UK: Polity.

———. 1987. *The Philosophical Discourse of Modernity* (trans. F. Lawrence). Cambridge, MA: MIT Press.

Hoselitz, B. 1960. *Sociological Aspects of Economic Growth*. New York: Free Press.

Kant, I. 1788/1949. *What Is Orientation in Thinking?* In *Critique of Practical Reason and Other Writings on Moral Philosophy* (trans. L. W. Beck). Chicago: University of Chicago Press.

Kumar, D. V. 2006. *Modernisation and Ethnicity*. New Delhi: Mittal Publications.

Lerner, D. 1958. *The Passing of Traditional Society*. New York: Free Press.

Levy, M. J. 1966. *Modernization and the Structure of Societies* (Vol. 1 and 2). Princeton, NJ: Princeton University Press.

Lyotard, J. F. 1984. *The Postmodern Condition*. Manchester, UK: Manchester University Press.

Marcuse, H. 1972. *One-dimensional Man*. London: Abacus.

McLennan, G. 1992. The Enlightenment Project revisited. In S. Hall, D. Helf & T. McGrew (eds), *Modernity and Its Futures* (pp. 327–377). Cambridge, UK: Polity.

Moore, B. 1967. *Social Origins of Dictatorship and Democracy: Lord and Peasant in the Making of the Modern World*. Harmondsworth, UK: Penguin.

Pandey, R. 1988. Studies of social change and development: Introduction. In R. Pandey (ed.), *Modernisation and Social Change* (pp. 1–16). New Delhi: Criterion Publications.

Parsons, T. 1964. Evolutionary universals in society. *American Sociological Review*, 29(3), 339–357.

Pathak, A. 1998. *Indian Modernity: Contradictions, Paradoxes and Possibilities*. New Delhi: Gyan Publishing.

Smelser, N. J. 1969. Mechanism of and adjustment to change. In T. Burns (ed.), *Industrial Man* (pp. 232–275). Harmondsworth, UK: Penguin.

Stephenson, J. B. 1968. Is everyone going modern? A critique and a for measuring modernism. *American Journal of Sociology*, 74(3), 35–47.

Touraine, A. 1995. *Critique of Modernity* (trans. David Macey). Malden, MA: Blackwell.

2

Contesting the European origins of modernity

Modernity has emerged as a dominant category to describe social transformations that have taken place and continue to take place for quite some time. Although modernity is being used extensively in social science literature, it continues to evade precise sociological understanding. What is modernity and how does one make sense of modernity are the issues that have been engaging the attention of social scientists for quite some time (e.g. see, Albrow 1996, Alexander 1996, Bauman 1991, 2000, Giddens 1990, Gupta 2011, Harvey 1989, Pathak 2006, Singh 1996). I have attempted to deal with these questions and the related issue of social change and development elsewhere (Kumar 2006, 2008, 2010, 2012). Let me briefly recapitulate. It was argued, in tune with what Callinicos said, that there are three distinct ways of looking at modernity: (i) as a philosophical idea, (ii) as a form of society and (iii) as an experience (Callinicos 1999, p. 297). As an *idea*, it represents a radical rupture with the past. It privileges progress, science, optimism and universality. It critiques superstitions, blind faiths and pessimism. As a form of society it may be characterized by distinctive economic, political and social characteristics. As an experience, it is full of contradictions. On one hand, it promises progress, happiness and advancement; on the other, it seeks to destroy everything we have and are known by. It introduces an element of uncertainty, risk and confusion.

What is common to these three categories is their Eurocentric proclivity. They all look at modernity as having emanated from Europe. The emergence of modernity was captured, as Bhambra argues, in terms of two aspects – rupture and difference (2007, p. 1). Rupture is understood in terms of a distinction between an agrarian past and modern industrial present and difference in terms of a distinction between Europe and the rest of the world. These two aspects were supposed to characterize modernity. Europe was said to have undergone modernization (modernity in action) from the fifteenth century, and it has been argued that this process would engulf the rest of the world sooner or later. Any society failing to become modern (if that is possible at all) would be regarded as 'deviant' in one sense or the other. What in essence this means is that the particularity of Europe gets privileged as the general and universal.

What this chapter seeks to do is that it goes beyond a mere descriptive account of the story of modernity and contests the widely accepted position that Europe was the *first* and *only* home of modernity. It is pertinent to mention here that there have been some notable attempts in this direction in the recent past (e.g. Bhambra 2007).

A number of social theorists have argued relentlessly that Europe was the home of modernity. Alexander, for example, argued, 'The transition to modernity within Western society provided "a capacity for transformation unprecedented in the other civilizations of the world"' (1995, p. 1). Similarly, Giddens, one of the most celebrated social theorists in the recent past, takes the position that modernity has its 'roots in specific characteristics of European history . . . [with] few parallels in prior periods or in other cultural settings' (1990, p. 174). Callinicos, the Marxist historian, looks at modernity as a specific kind of idea associated with a specific kind of society – the modern West (1999). Even postmodernist theorists such as Seidman, who are otherwise supposed to be sceptical of any form of certainty, argue that modernity needs to be located in the distinctiveness of the culture of the modern West.

Recently there have been some attempts to counter such a Eurocentric, hegemonic and homogenizing construction of modernity pursuant to making a contestable claim that 'modernity' emerged from Europe. Conceptual categories such as multiple modernities, global modernities and hybrid and entangled modernities have been used to provide an alternative perspective on modernity (Comaroff and Comaroff 1993, pp. 1–18). However, the problem with these categories is that they do not question the 'fact' of modernity having emerged in the West (Bhambra 2007, p. 6). The West is seen as the original birthplace of modernity and modernity has travelled from the West to other parts of the world. Delanty, for example, argues that modernity emerged first in Europe and then spread to other parts of the world that have tried to adapt themselves to modernity depending on their local traditions (2006, pp. 266–278). In the process they have tried to extricate themselves from the imprint of modernity that emerged in Europe. According to Bhambra, 'The concept of modernity, abstracted from its inflections or not, nonetheless remains tied to what is generally understood as the European experience' (2007, p. 6). Therefore, even these categories are not adequate in appreciating the varied and rich experience of modernity. Reducing it to only a European experience does not do justice to the richness of the origin of modernity. We need to go beyond these categories too to be able to do that.

Contesting the Eurocentric perspective

Why is it necessary to question the 'fact' that modernity had originated in Europe alone? It becomes necessary to do so because the supposedly founding moments of modernity – the Renaissance, the French Revolution and Industrial Revolutions – that had taken place in Europe making it the 'supposed' birth place of modernity, after all, became what they were because of the support from rich and varied non-European sources. The contribution of non-West sources to these events has been ignored, perhaps intentionally if one may add. Furthermore, the transition of so-called modernity from the West to the non-West occurred essentially through colonial encounters, a fact that has been conveniently ignored. In the sociological accounts of modernity, one does not find sufficient mention of the role of colonialism in the transition of modernity from the West to other parts of the world. This is despite that fact that colonial encounters have been a particularly painful experience for many.

Let us take a look at each of these events. Since the three most supposedly momentous events – the Renaissance, the French Revolution and Industrial Revolutions – that symbolize modernity occurred in Europe, it was argued that modernity began only from Europe. Questions regarding the contribution of other civilizations to modernity and the impact of colonial encounters on the non-West were completely ignored (Bhambra 2007). I will now try and deconstruct these events to show that Europe cannot possibly claim exclusive authorship of modernity.

The Renaissance understood in terms of rebirth was supposed to represent one of the key moments in modernity, and, since it took place in Europe, the natural corollary was that Europe became the birth place of modernity. As Toulmin argued, 'Renaissance was evidently a transitional phase, in which the seeds of Modernity germinated and grew' (1990, p. 23). For many historians, 'the significance of the Renaissance was that it was the beginning of the modern world' (Burke 1964, p. 133). It was during this period that scholars were believed to have begun their journey of contemplating about the human condition and about humanism in general. That is the reason why activities connected with such contemplation became part of what came to be known as 'humanities'. The strong belief was that the ancient texts had a wealth of wisdom to offer, and it was through a creative and critical engagement with those texts that an appropriate understanding of the present could be obtained. Scholars such as Dante, Boccaccio and others were supposed to have inaugurated such a literary renaissance. These scholars were believed to have made tenacious attempts to learn what they could from great minds such as Plato and Aristotle by examining ancient texts. The wealth of wisdom generated in the ancient period was said to be lost during the medieval period (the Dark Age). However, the point to be noted here is that the Renaissance scholars also wanted to move beyond what the ancient texts had to offer and develop new and alternative ways of understanding the present. They were attempting to create and implement new modes of thinking to enrich life in the present. They were not keen on repeating what was said in ancient texts; clearly, they were striving for something that was distinctive. As Ferguson contended, 'The Renaissance was conceived as a period in the history of European civilization, a period with a distinctive spirit, sharply contrasted with that of the Middle ages' (1948, p. 177). Tenacious efforts of Renaissance scholars were believed to have resulted in significant advances in literature, art, architecture, science and geography. These advances were seen be to be responsible for a shift from their veneration of the ancient texts to a feeling of superiority over them (see Butzer 1992). The distinctive strands present within the Renaissance, such as the discovery of the ancient texts, development of historical consciousness and humanism, vast improvements in the arts and science together with the discovery of the 'New' world made the Renaissance a very distinctive phase in the development of European history. This was supposed to have heralded the birth of modernity in Europe.

It was only much later that the uniqueness of the Renaissance began to be seriously questioned and also the idea that Europe was the first and the only home of modernity. Scholars such as Kristeller argued that Renaissance, which was supposed to have heralded modernity in Europe by distinguishing itself from the medieval (dark) age, also contained some medieval traits (1974). Also, presence of earlier renaissances, such as the Carolingian or twelfth-century renaissance within Europe, deeply problematized the uniqueness of Renaissance (Sanford 1951, Sullivan 1989). Furthermore, taking an objection to the uniqueness of Renaissance and to the lack of any mention of contribution of Islamic scholars to the growth of humanities, Sabra argues that these scholars were equally, if not more, driven by the concerns of Renaissance and those of later Humanist thinkers (1984, p. 138). The intellectual contributions of Islamic scholars to learning and knowledge within Europe and their role transmitting writings of ancient civilizations such as Greek, Roman and Oriental have been widely recognized (Bernal 1987, Kraemer 1984). As far as improvements in arts were concerned, it was believed that such improvements were a result of travel only within Europe. Artists travelling within Europe, it was assumed, only contributed to the refining of techniques in arts. As Bhambra points out, the editors of a recent collection of reprints maintain that between 1400 and 1700 there were over 250 descriptions of Egypt by Western scholars suggesting that travels to Egypt were at least as common as those to Greece (2007, p. 97). What this clearly shows is that improvements in arts were effected as a result of travels not only within Europe but also between Europe and other parts, contesting the idea that Renaissance was an exclusively European affair. Even the Western science, which was claimed to be essentially an endogenous affair, was in fact influenced by non-Western sources. For example, Copernicus's mathematical astronomy drew heavily from Islamic scholars such as Nasir ad-Din at-Tusi and Ibn ash Shatir (Bernal 1987, p. 156). The advantage that Copernicus perhaps had was that he had better access to texts as compared to his predecessors. What is missing in the account of Renaissance is the role of printing press, which itself originated in China, in transmitting the cultural essence of Renaissance. The printing press was carried to Europe in the Middle Ages by the Arabs, a fact that does not find any mention in the modernist accounts of Renaissance (Gilmore 1952, p. 187). This facilitated a shift from a scribal to a typographical culture producing fundamental changes in the prevailing intellectual models of continuity and change (Bhambra 2007, p. 97). What has really happened is that in an account of birth and growth of modernity, Europe privileged itself and the 'Other' (the non-West and non-Europe) has been systematically written out. It was much later that the dominant discourse that is found in sociological accounts about modernity having first originated in Europe began to be contested by the historically inclined sociologists.

Another momentous event that was used to claim that modernity emerged in Europe was the French Revolution. As the French Revolution led to the emergence of the nation-state that represents the political project of modernity, it has been emphasized that modernity took birth in Europe first. Furet refers to the role of French Revolution in inventing the political form of modernity or, more succinctly, 'the empirical modality through which the world of free and equal individuals has made its appearance in our history' (1988, p. 18). This event, that is, the French Revolution, was seen as something that marked the advent of something unique and extraordinary; in short, the advent of modern political society. Nation-state became a reality following the French Revolution. There have been debates whether nations are modern or they had been present in the pre-modern times in the form of ethnies (Smith 1986). I have dealt with this elsewhere (Kumar 2010). We will not pursue it here. Apart from engendering the nation-state, what the French Revolution was said to have done was that it created representative institutions, a Constitution, the Declaration of the Rights of Man and the Citizen, and the Decree of 11th August abolishing feudalism. After taking birth in Europe, the nation-state which was the political form of modernity became global. It was argued that the spread of nation-state to the non-European world was part of a natural progression of world history. This account conveniently ignores the process through which the political form of modernity, that is, nation-state, got transmitted. History would tell us that it was essentially through colonial encounters, which were basically hegemonic and violent, that the nation-state spread to other parts of the world. Thus, as Chatterjee argues, the issue of nation-state in the non-European world has to be understood as historically fused with colonialism (1986, p. 30). Any discussion of the spread of nation-state must include the question of colonialism. Otherwise that discussion would be devoid of factual background and intellectual strength. It was because of colonial encounters that the nation-state spread to various parts of the world. It also needs to be mentioned here that some of the 'modern' political and governmental measures were first initiated in the colonies and exported to the West. Fingerprinting, just to give one such example, was first used by the colonial government in Bengal, India, as a 'scientific' means to locating an individual (Cohn and Dirks 1988, pp. 224–228). Furthermore, as Viswanathan points out, it was in the colonies that the English literature was first introduced as a subject in the curriculum before it was given that status in the home country (1989, p. 3). The point one wishes to make here is that the transmission of the nation-state seen as modern was not a natural progression as has been emphasized by the theorists of modernity. Rather, it should be closely seen in conjunction with what was happening simultaneously, that is, the spread of colonialism in the non-European world.

Yet another event that was supposed to have heralded the birth of modernity in Europe was the Industrial Revolution. The Industrial Revolution, which was said to have gained momentum between 1750 and 1850, was believed to have produced a 'radical shift in the structure of the economy, in the composition of total output, and in the distribution of employment' (Harwell 1965, p. 181), leading to the engendering of a distinct type of economy not seen previously. It constitutes a rupture between the traditional economy and the modern industrial economy. Since it was said to have occurred in Europe first, it came to be logically implied that modernity began its journey from Europe. The factors said to be responsible for the occurrence of the Industrial Revolution are growth of urban centres, commercial agriculture, technological innovations, spread of banking and finance, and a significant rise in population. In conjunction with each other they were said to have contributed to the process of industrialization. Any society failing to become industrialized is considered deviant and viewed as being unable to solve problems such as low standard of life, illiteracy, ill-health and ignorance present in that society. Thus, the spread of industrialization to other parts is seen as a natural and inevitable process. What this account conveniently effaces is the existence of colonial and unequal trading relations characterizing the West and the non-West (Bhambra 2007, p. 125). This shortcoming, however, is sought be rectified to some extent by theorists such as Wallerstein, Frank and others. Wallerstein argued that the emergence of 'industrial capitalism' should be explained not only in terms of the factors mentioned previously but also in terms of the incorporation of non-capitalist systems and continuous exploitation of their resources for the development of capitalist systems (1979). Contrary to the widely accepted perception that the success of industrial capitalism in Britain is endogenously created, achieved and maintained, some scholars looked at the impact of de-industrialization of countries like India on the success of British industry (Washbrook 1997). Any explanation of the success of industrialization in Europe in general must take into account the story of underdevelopment in the rest of the world. Otherwise, such an explanation would be empirically poor and historically untenable. As Eric Williams's (1994) brilliant account shows the 'triangular trade' between Britain and France and Africa and colonial America was an important source of capital accumulation that finally led to the financing of the Industrial Revolution. He argues, 'The slave ships sailed from the home country with a cargo of manufactured goods. These were exchanged at a profit on the coast of Africa for Negroes, who were traded on the plantations, at another profit, in exchange for a cargo of colonial produce to be taken back to the home country' (1994, pp. 51–52). Theorists such as Samir Amin (1977) and Andre Gunder Frank (1975, pp. 386–393) give us powerful arguments why the process of industrialization should not be viewed purely as an endogenous affair to Europe. Frank, for example, argues, 'The conditions for the rise of the West to hegemony and the transition to capitalism in Europe cannot be found within Europe alone: they have to be sought in the world as a whole' (1992, p. 390). Fundamentally, the logical point is that if world system has to be taken as a given fact, why should Europe be taken as the centre of the world? One cannot simply ignore the considerable scholarly work carried out to study the long history of complex interconnections and negotiations between people across both sea and land (e.g. Das Gupta 1985, Perlin 1994, Subrahmanyam 1988). The essential point that emerges is that the development of any socioeconomic process in any part of the world should not be seen as an isolated affair. The network of relations across the globe that has been a historical fact needs to be factored into account as the main cause of the advent of modernity.

The main burden of argument ably advanced by some of the social theorists such as Bhambra in the recent past is that privileging Europe as the home of modernity, without considering the contribution of other parts of the world, as we have seen above, is deeply problematic. The histories of imperialism, colonialism and slavery need to be given due attention in accounting for the growth and spread of modernity (Bhambra 2007, p. 145). It is these histories that enabled Europe and the West to achieve modernity. The multiple forms of engagement between Europe and other parts of the world need to be recognized in any account of growth of modernity in Europe.

The search for an authentic origin of modernity is an extremely arduous, and, if I may say, a meaningless task, because of the complex nature of interconnections and relations that evolved over a long period between different parts of the world. What was said to have been European in origin could have been borrowed from any part of the world – Asia, Africa and so on, illustrations of which were given previously. Because of the hegemony that Europe enjoyed, intellectual or otherwise, over the rest of the world, it has been able to hegemonize the debate about the origin of modernity. Bhambra nicely captures the contours of such a debate in the following words, 'When it was "proved" that someone else had invented it, the origin rested in the application of a thing (e.g. the invention of the printing press is attributed to the Chinese but claimed as European as a consequence of its replication). When it was "proved" that someone else had also used it, then origin rested in the mass application of a thing (e.g. factory production of cotton). When it was "proved" that someone else had also mass produced it, the origin rested in the claim to have done it first. First and alone' (2007, p. 150).

The fact of modernity having emerged in Europe first and alone needs to be problematized. The notion of 'connected histories' (Subrahmanyam 1997) enables us to have a better appreciation of the trajectory that modernity has traversed. It is a valuable analytical tool to understand and locate the growth of modernity. This takes into account the contribution of other civilizations and societies to the advent of modernity and seeks to delegitimize the European hegemonic idea that modernity emerged there 'first and alone'. A more detailed treatment of the idea of 'connected histories' will be undertaken in due course.

REFERENCES

Albrow, M. 1996. *The Global Age: State and Society beyond Modernity*. Cambridge, UK: Polity.

Alexander, J. C. 1995. *Social Theory: Relativism, Reduction and the Problem of Reason*. London: Verso.

———. 1996. Critical reflections on reflexive modernisation. *Theory, Culture and Society*, 13(4), 133–138.

Amin, S. 1977. Accumulation and development: A theoretical model. *Review of African Political Economy*, 1(43), 9–26.

Bauman, Z. 1991. *Modernity and Ambivalence*. Cambridge, UK: Polity.

———. 2000. *Liquid Modernity*. Cambridge, UK: Polity.

Bernal, M. 1987. *Black Athena: The Afroasiatic Roots Classical Civilisation. Volume I: The Fabrication of Ancient Greece 1785–1987*. London: Free Association Books.

Bhambra, G. K. 2007. *Rethinking Modernity: Postcolonialism and the Sociological Imagination*. New York: Palgrave Macmillan.

Burke, P. 1964. *The Renaissance*. London: Longman.

Butzer, K. W. 1992. From Columbus to Acosta: Science, geography, and the new world – Annals of the Association of American Geographers: The Americas before and after 1492. *Current Geographical Research*, 82(3), 543–565.

Callinicos, A . 1999. *Social Theory: A Historical Introduction*. Cambridge, UK: Polity.

Chatterjee, P. 1986. *Nationalist Thought and the Colonial World: A Derivative Discourse*. London: Zed Books.

Cohn, B. S. & Dirks, N. B. 1988. Beyond the fringe: The nation-state, colonialism, and the technologies of power. *Journal of Historical Sociology*, 1(2), 243–256.

Comaroff, J. & Comaroff, J. 1993. Introduction. In J. Comaroff & J. Comaroff (eds), *Modernity and Its Malcontents: Ritual and Power in Postcolonial Africa* (pp. 67–85). Chicago: University of Chicago Press.

Das Gupta, A. 1985. Indian merchants and the Western Indian Ocean: The early seventeenth century. *Modern Asian Studies*, 19(3), 481–499.

Delanty, G. 2006. Modernity and the escape from Eurocentrism. In G. Delanty (ed.), *Handbook of Contemporary European Social Theory* (pp. 123–155). London: Routledge.

Ferguson, W. K. 1948. *The Renaissance in Historical Thought: Five Centuries of Interpretation*. Cambridge, MA: Riverside Press.

Frank, A. G. 1975. *On Capitalist Underdevelopment*. Bombay: Oxford University Press.

———. 1992. Fourteen ninety-two once again. *Political Geography*, 11(4), 123–136.

Furet, F. 1988. *Marx and the French Revolution* (trans. D. K. Furet). Chicago: Chicago University Press.

Giddens, A. 1990. *The Consequences of Modernity*. Cambridge, UK: Polity.

Gilmore, M. P. 1952. *The World of Humanism 1453–1517*. New York: Harper and Row.

Gupta, D. 2011. *Mistaken Modernity: India between Worlds*. New Delhi: HarperCollins.

Harvey, D. 1989. *The Condition of Postmodernity*. Oxford, UK: Blackwell.

Harwell, R. M. 1965. The causes of the industrial revolution: An essay in methodology. *The Economic History Review: Essays in Economic History*, 18(1), 164–182.

Kraemer, J. I. 1984. Humanism in the renaissance of Islam: A preliminary study. *Journal of the American Oriental Society: Studies in Islam and the Ancient Near East Dedicated to Franz Rosenthal*, 104(1), 7–30.

Kristeller, P. O. 1974. *Medieval Aspects of Renaissance Learning* (ed. and trans. E. P. Mahoney). Durham, NC: Duke University Press.

Kumar, D. V. 2006. *Modernisation and Ethnicity*. New Delhi: Mittal Publications.

———. 2008. Engaging with modernity: Need for a critical negotiation. *Sociological Bulletin*, 57(2), 240–254.

———. 2010. Gellnerian theory of nation and nationalism: A critical appraisal. *Sociological Bulletin*, 59(3), 392–406.

———. 2012. *Social Change and Development*. Jaipur: Rawat Publications.

Pathak, A. 2006. *Modernity, Globalisation and Identity: Towards a Reflexive Quest*. New Delhi: Aakar Books.

Perlin, F. 1994. *Unbroken Landscape: Commodity, Category, Sign and Identity: Their Production as Myth and Knowledge from 1500*. Hampshire, UK: Variorum.

Sabra, A. I. 1984. The Andalusian revolt against Ptolemaic astronomy: Averroes and al-Bitruji. In E. Mendelsohn (ed.), *Transformation and Tradition in the Sciences: Essays in Honour of I. Bernard Cohen* (pp. 133–154). Cambridge, UK: Cambridge University Press.

Sanford, E. M. 1951. The twelfth century – renaissance or proto-renaissance. *Speculu*, 26(4), 635–642.

Singh, Y. 1996. *Modernisation of Indian Tradition*. Jaipur: Rawat Publications.

Smith, A. D. 1986. *The Ethnic Origins of Nations*. Oxford, UK: Blackwell.

Subrahmanyam, S. 1988. Persians, pilgrims and Portuguese: The travails of Masulipatnam shipping in the Western Indian Ocean, 1590–1665. *Modern Asian Studies*, 22(3), 503–530.

———. 1997. Connected histories: Notes towards a reconfiguration of early modern Eurasia. *Modern Asian Studies*, 31(3), 735–762.

Sullivan, R. E. 1989. The Carolingian age: Reflections on its place in the history of the Middle Ages. *Speculu*, 64(2), 267–306.

Toulmin, S. E. 1990. *Cosmopolis: The Hidden Agenda of Modernity*. New York: Free Press.

Viswanathan, G. 1989. *Masks of Conquest: Literary Study and British Rule in India*. New York: Columbia University Press.

Wallerstein, I. 1979. *The Capitalist World-Economy: Essays*. Cambridge, UK: Cambridge University Press.

Washbrook, D. A. 1997. From comparative sociology to global history: Britain and India in the pre-history of modernity. *Journal of Economic and Social History of the Orient*, 40(4), 410–443.

Williams, E. 1994. *Capitalism and Slavery*. Chapel Hill, NC: University of North Carolina Press.

3

Modernization and ethnicity

Interrogating different theoretical perspectives

There is a scholarly body of literature on the relationship between modernization and ethnicity. Some of the classical sociologists (Marx, Durkheim, for example) emphasized the decline of ethnicity in the context of modernization, though the exact reasons they have given for the decline are different. Others arguing on the basis of considerable body of evidence have sought to prove that the assumption that ethnicity would decline in the face of modernization is baseless and unfounded. They draw our attention to the instances of ethnic resurgence not only in the so-called traditional societies but also in the 'supposedly' advanced and modern societies. For example, one can notice enhanced ethnic assertiveness not only in countries like India, Sri Lanka and so on but also in Canada, France, Yugoslavia, Britain and America. Even the contemporary process of globalization has not supplanted the significance of ethnicity, as reflected in the growing incidence of ethnic conflicts.

Those who argue for the decline of ethnicity in the context of modernization do so for different reasons. One can divide them into two broad categories: Marxist expectancy and liberal expectancy (Fenton 1999, p. 96).

And those who argue for the persistence of ethnicity do so again for different reasons. One can divide them into two categories: primordialists and instrumentalists. Briefly stated, the former argue that ethnicity holds ineffable affective significance for its members and, therefore, it will continue to exercise its influence, modernization or no modernization. The latter argue that ethnicity is used as an effective instrument to achieve some common purpose. Therefore, the form of ethnicity may change depending on the context, but its significance will continue; in fact, the significance of ethnicity has only gone up in the modern world.

I, therefore, propose to undertake an examination of studies about the relationship between modernization and ethnicity on the basis of the framework given as follows:

Figure 1 Relationship between modernization and ethnicity

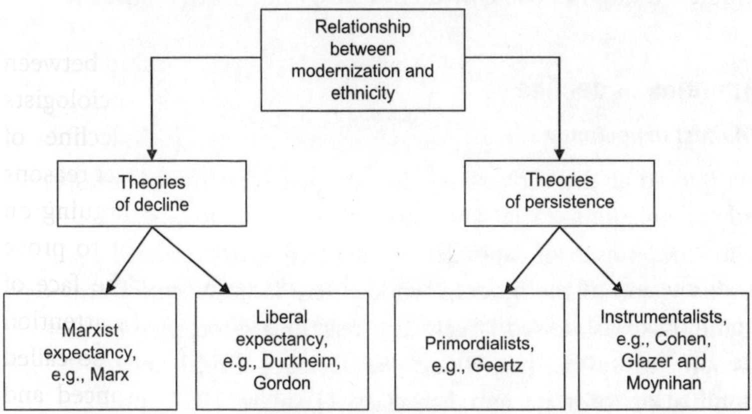

In my view, the aforesaid framework has both advantages and disadvantages. Its chief advantage lies in the fact that it will enable us to arrange numerous scholarly works on the relationship between modernization and ethnicity in a systematic and meaningful way. However, its main disadvantage is that it will not enable us to appreciate the subtleties that are associated with each study. For example, some studies can be unambiguously described as primordialist and some as instrumentalist. However, there are some cases where an apparently instrumentalist position does in fact view ethnicity as containing an element of primordialism. Nevertheless, I believe this will provide a good starting point to look at the various studies that examine the relationship between modernization and ethnicity. If the reader finds that there is a misinterpretation of a particular study, please correct me, because such omissions are mine alone.

One point needs to be mentioned at this juncture. Some studies have directly problematized the relationship between modernization and ethnicity. Others have done it by implication. However, such studies also give us valuable insights into their relationship. It will be in the fitness of things if I make another point clear. I am interested only in those studies that look at the relationship between modernization and ethnicity either directly or indirectly. Therefore, I do not propose to review those studies that focus on ethnicity per se or modernization per se. This may force me to leave out many studies, though valuable by themselves, from my examination.

Theories of decline

Marxist expectancy

As quoted at the very outset, Marx argues that the importance of ethnic, religious, racial and nationalistic attachments will decline with the growth of capitalism (a modern socioeconomic system). In his vision of the modern world, there is no place for ethnicity. Nationalism is viewed largely as a reactionary force, an ideological weapon meant to perpetuate the social, political and economic domination of the capitalist class (Tishkov 1997, p. 42). The interests of the exploited labouring classes lie in transcending local particularisms and nationalism by uniting as an international class of workers.

In the Marxist theorization, class would assume central importance. Class relations are transformed by the revolutionary forces of capitalism. These class relations are founded upon the exploitation of labour by capital and the inevitability of the search for profit. The economic tendencies or laws of capitalism provoke recurring crises in the sustainability of capitalism as an economic system: the growth of class consciousness and organization provokes political challenges to the capitalist state. All these challenges will replace capitalism with socialism. A new economic organization will be dedicated to social production for use rather than profit.

However, for Marx there are two points of entry for an interest in ethnicity. The first is that nationalism and ethno-national sentiments are viewed as distractions from the development of a rational class consciousness, the political formation which hastens the demise of capitalism. The second point is that ethnicity is seen as having ideological and political functions within capitalism, specifically as a form of consciousness that divides and, therefore weakens, working-class consciousness and organization (Balibar and Wallerstein 1991, p.102).

However, ethnic consciousness will have to give way to class consciousness with the inexorable intensification of class contradictions. The very logic of capitalism demands that particularistic attachments should have no place and class conflicts become the primary force of societal changes. As capitalism develops, so does class consciousness, allying men and women on a rational basis to those whose material circumstances they share. When capitalism is transcended by socialism then will begin the building of a rational civil society in which men and women could relate to each other free of the encumbrances of class and birth. However, for that reason those who saw themselves as building socialist states found it hard to cope with the 'nationalistic loyalties, sentiments and collectivities' (Diamond and Plattner 1994, Kupchan 1995). Political ideology demands that particularistic forms ought to diminish, whereas political realities indicate that identities remain.

In the recent past, there have been influential studies within the tradition of Marxism, some arguing that ethnic and racial relations should be viewed as camouflaging exploitative class relations, and racial differentiation is always created in the context of class differentiation, thus giving primacy to the analysis of class structure. Others have taken the position (which can be regarded as an internal critique of Marxism) that ethnic and racial relations should be viewed as being relatively autonomous from class relations (Gilroy 1987, Miles 1984, Solomos and Back 1995).

Liberal expectancy

According to the liberal expectancy view, decline of ethnicity is inevitable. This argument is contextualized in terms of the goings-on in economic, political, social and cultural spheres. In the economic sphere, growth of meritocracy renders redundant particularistic attachments such as ethnic attachments. Economic positions are acquired on the basis of merit rather than on the basis of birth. In the political sphere, ethnicity will no longer be relevant to civic status. The principles of liberty, equality and justice, which are considered universalistic in spirit, will undermine the dominance of any one ethnic group. In the social sphere, it is argued that formal associations supplant allegiance found on kinship and communal membership ascribed at birth. In Durkheim's language, the natal milieu, the sphere of social ties associated with birth, progressively diminishes in importance. In the cultural sphere, world trade and mass communication are seen as solvents of local cultures and harbingers of a certain cultural uniformity that undermines ethnic diversity. These global influences are the suggested source of homogenization.

The most unmistakable argument for the decline of ethnicity is to be found in the liberal-universalist sociology of Emile Durkheim. His argument centres upon what he calls the decline of the natal milieu – the locale and social obligations – especially of family, into which an individual is born. The belief that particularistic ties should decline is an element of liberal democratic ideology: the belief that they will decline is part of the sociology of modernization. Durkheim viewed the French Revolution as the beginning of the redefinition of people as citizens, setting in train the development of laws and social institutions that recognized the freedom and dignity of the individual (Tiryakan 1971, p. 68). He viewed 'race' and ethnic origin as declining facets of the modern social order, precisely because both were rooted in birth (Fenton 1999, p. 100).

With respect to ethnicity his most telling remarks were with respect to Jewishness in France. An atheist Jew himself, he thought that the kind of ties represented by an ethnic community such as Jews would decline in significance in the modern state of citizens. Significantly he stressed that his defence of Dreyfus and his critique of the persecutors of Dreyfus, a Jewish military captain falsely convicted by treason in a wave of anti-Semitic politics, was above all a defence of the rights of men, of liberty and of dignity of the individual (Fenton 1999, p. 100).

Milton Gordon makes a similar point. He expects that the kinds of features that divide one group from another will inevitably lose their weight and sharpness in modern and modernizing societies, there will be increasing emphasis on achievement rather than ascription, common systems of education and communication would level differences and nationally uniform economic and political systems will prevail. Under these circumstances, the primordial differences between groups would be expected to assume lesser importance (Gordon 1975). One can also refer to Karl Deutsch (1953) in this connection.

There are broadly two approaches that enable us to explain the persistence of ethnicity even in the context of modernization. They are primordial and instrumental (also referred to as 'circumstantial approaches'; Banks 1996, p. 39).

Theories of persistence

Primordial approach

The primordialist approach holds that ethnicity is an innate aspect of human identity. It is a given, requiring description rather than explanation. It holds tremendous emotional significance for the members of the group. Because of its primordial nature, it is bound to persist even in the context of modernization.

We can now proceed to review some of those studies that are primordialist in orientation.

Edward Shils seems to have been one of the first to use the term 'primordial', in reference to the relationships within the family. In his view, the relational attachment to a kin member is not merely to the other family members as a person but as a possessor of certain especially significant relational qualities, which could only be described as 'primordial' (1957, p. 142). This attachment is not cemented through interaction; rather, it derives its strength from 'a certain ineffable significance – attributed to the tie of blood' (p. 142). He perceives ethnic ties as an extension of kinship ties and attributes primordiality to them exactly the same way he does to kinship ties. The attribution of primordiality to ethnic ties may logically imply that the forces of modernization have no influence on ethnic attachments. Thus, ethnic ties just as the kinship ties would persist even in the context of modernization.

Fredrick Barth's edited book *Ethnic Groups and Boundaries* (1969) proved to be enormously influential in shaping the ideas about ethnic groups. The book contains short essays by Scandinavian anthropologists, each concerned with the 'social organization of culture difference' and analyses data from Norway, North-East Africa, Mexico, Pakistan and Laos. It needs to be recognized that the chief impact was made not so much by the studies themselves as by Barth's introductory essay. Banks considers Barth as belonging to the group of primordialists (1996, p. 39).

The whole burden of his argument is that an ethnic group needs to be understood not in terms of objective features such as dress, language and so on its members share but in terms of boundaries. He makes two significant points. First, the group may lose some of these features and acquire new ones over a period of time but the boundaries might persist despite a flow of personnel and information across them. Second, and, as a corollary to the first, such groups cannot exist in isolation but only in contrast to other such groups; that is, the boundary does not bind 'something off from nothingness, but rather it distinguishes between two (or more) "somethings"' (Barth 1969, pp. 14–15).

Barth argues that ethnicity is a superordinate identity, one that transcends or is at least equivalent to all other identities (such as those based on gender or status); as such his position is closer to that of primordialist ethnicity as a permanent and essential condition: 'the constraints on person's behaviour which spring from his ethnic identity . . . tend to be absolute' (1969, p. 17). In other words, so long as ethnic groups exist ethnicity will exist.

However, the person who is most clearly identified with primordialism is Clifford Geertz (Geertz, 1973). Geertz says ethnicity is 'primordial' and defines primordiality, which is worth quoting at length, as follows:

> By a primordial attachment [it] is meant [as] one that stems from the "givens" of existence, or, more precisely, since culture is inevitably involved in such matters, the assumed "givens" of social existence, immediate contiguity and live connection mainly, but beyond them the givenness that stems from being born into a particular religious community, speaking a particular language or even dialect of a language, and following particular social practices. These contiguities of blood, speech, custom and so on are seen to have an ineffable, and at times, overpowering, coerciveness in and of themselves. One is bound to one's kinsman, one's neighbour, one's fellow believer, ipso facto, as a result not merely of personal moral obligation, but at least in great part, by virtue of some unaccountable import attributed to the very tie itself. (1973, p. 45)

Thus, ethnicity holds tremendous ineffable and affective significance for the members of a group who share language, culture and so on. Ethnicity does not arise out of personal attraction, tactical necessity or communal interests. However, his definition is viewed as a mixture of relatively precise sociological conceptualization and ideological mystification (Rex 1986, p. 188). The issue that remains unresolved in his definition is that we replace the ties that are given to us in our families of birth by others that we choose. In doing so, we may identity with an increasingly wide range of other ties. What needs to be explained is the extension of the feeling of original ethnic bondedness to a wide range of persons and into adult life. Others who subscribe to this perspective would include Bromley (1974), Epstein (1958), Isaacs (1975), Parming and Cheung (1980), Stack (1986) and Tambs-Lynche (1980).

The instrumental position

The instrumental or the circumstantial approach holds that ethnicity is an artefact, created by individuals or groups to bring together a group of people for some common purpose. It is used as an instrument to mobilize the members of a group to achieve socioeconomic and political objectives.

It would be clear from the above view that primordial approach seeks psychological explanation for the behavioural phenomenon of ethnic solidarity whereas the circumstantial approach prefers a behavioural explanation. The proponents of each approach have tended to argue that the other is restricted to the range of ethnic behaviours it can explain. The problem with the primordial approach, the circumstantialists argue, is that while it can explain the persistence of ethnic identity over time, it cannot address the issue of why such identity can and indeed often does change or fluctuate in its intensity as well as differentially distributed at a given moment of time throughout a single group – a deficiency that they believe is remedied by their focus on social circumstances surrounding this identity or rather on changing or differential social circumstances. In other words, they argue that a constant cannot explain a variable. The primordialists for their part contend that while circumstantialists can explain why ethnicity fluctuates over time they are less able to account for the fact that despite its temporal fluctuations, ethnicity often persists, sometimes over centuries; changing circumstances can explain the fluctuation but only primordial sentiments can account for its persistence. In other words, primordialists argue that a variable cannot explain a constant.

I will now proceed to examine some studies associated with instrumental position and, furthermore, take up some related approaches such as rational choice, optional-situational and oppositional approaches for a brief examination. The last approach, that is, the oppositional approach, is said to provide the basis for the synthesis of primordial approach with instrumental approach.

It needs to be reiterated here that an examination of all these approaches may lead to the logical conclusion that ethnicity will persist even in the context of modernization as it serves certain instrumental purposes.

One of the most pronounced instrumentalist positions has been taken by Abner Cohen. The whole burden of Cohen's argument presented in his *Custom and Politics in Urban Africa* (1969) is that ethnicity is instrumental; that is, the reasons for the assertion of an ethnic identity by a group are essentially economic and political rather than psychological. Thus, his position is clearly anti-primordialist. He demonstrates this with a study of Hausa traders who are involved in the trade of kola nuts and cattle in the city of Ibadan, in the south-western Nigeria. The assertion of ethnic identity among the Hausas is relatively recent, say from 1950s. He identifies two factors as being responsible for the strong ethnicity of the Hausas in Ibadan. First, there are internal causes that revolve around the need to maintain a monopoly of the Kola nut and cattle traders. Hausa traders in Ibadan (where they are producers) send kola nuts (which are chewed as a stimulant and much used throughout West Africa) to Hausa traders in the north where they are in heavy demand (1969, p. 131). Conversely, the cattle are sent to the South for consumption there. It serves their business interests best if they use ethnic networks to control their end of the two trades. Second, there are external causes. There has been a certain amount of erosion in the political autonomy of Ibadan (which was there during the indirect colonial rule) following the blossoming of Nigerian national politics (an illustration of modernization). As a response to this they defined and asserted their ethnic identity. He uses the expression 'Retribalization' to describe this process.

Daniel Bell, an incredibly perceptive sociologist, has identified certain social and political trends that have given rise to predominance of ethnicity in the so-called modern world (Bell 1975, pp. 141–174). First, the growing tendency towards more inclusive identities manifested more recently in the globalization of economy and culture has immeasurably affected certain primordial attachments such as kinship, tribe ethnic group and so on from which individuals used to derive their psychological anchorages. In these circumstances one would expect the rise of parochial forces to provide emotions, and ethnicity is one of them. Second, the increasing politicization of the decisions that affect the communal lives of persons makes the need for group organization more necessary, and ethnic grouping becomes a ready means of demanding group rights or providing defence against other groups. Third, the inexorable breakup of traditional authority structures and previous affective social units – nations and class – has made ethnic attachment more salient. The diverse pressures that the nation is being subjected to have made it considerably weak. Similarly, class ceased to be a revolutionary force, as predicted by Marx, as a result of introduction of welfare measures by both the developed world and now the developing world.

Why should ethnicity become prominent? Why not other categories such as class? The reason, as he suggested, is ethnicity can combine an affective tie with an interest. What groups such as class which speak of only objective material interests lack are emotions and affective ties. Similarly, groups that harp only on emotional ties cannot be salient because interests that provide sustaining power to such groups are absent. In contrast, ethnic groups successfully combine an affective tie with an interest.

One can notice an attempt on the part of Bell to transcend the primordialist and instrumentalist debate. At the same time the instrumentalist perspective seems more predominant as he stresses the point that ethnic grouping becomes vital in demanding rights and privileges.

Glazer and Moynihan in their highly influential work *Beyond the Melting Pot* (1970), a study of ethnic groups in New York City, attempted to demolish the hypothesis that ethnicity was disappearing. It was thought that 'assimilation' or 'Americanization' of immigrants was only a matter of time as all identities would meet. However, the argument put forward by Glazer and Moynihan that identities had not disappeared but instead were asserting themselves had refuted the melting-pot hypothesis.

They made their instrumentalist position absolutely clear in their 1975 collection of essays *Ethnicity: Theory and Experience*. In the 'Introduction' to the essays, they argued that ethnic conflicts (an expression of enhanced ethnicity) have only increased in intensity in the last decade or so (1975, p. 6). Examples are conflicts between Anglophone and Francophone in Canada, Catholic and Protestants in North Ireland, Chinese and Malay in Malaysia, and so on. They basically offer two reasons for this.

The first is the evolution of the welfare state in the more advanced economies of the world and the advance of socialist state in underdeveloped economies. The state becomes a crucial and direct arbiter of economic well-being as well as of political status and whatever flows from that in both circumstances. As a matter of strategic efficiency it is not beneficial to assert claims on the basis of a very general category such as workers, peasants, while-collar employees and so on. Any party doing that would not be able to reap rich political benefits. On the other hand asserting claims on behalf of an ethnic group that is supposed to combine an affective tie with an interest makes a lot of political sense. It would help a political party to reap rich political harvest.

The second reason is the determination of every group to assert its own norms against the norms of other and dominant groups. Here the influence of Ralf Dahrendorf is unmistakable. Success of an individual and, by extension, of the group is determined by various factors. In this respect all individuals and all groups do not experience equal amount of achievement. Groups that are left behind distance themselves and assert their own distinct norms. This is where immense possibilities for ethnic groups to become salient exist. Giving the example of India, they say that language conflicts in India today have little to do with the right to the public use of language, as did so many struggles of the nineteenth century when, for example, there were efforts to 'Russify' the Russian Empire. Today they have more to do with which language user shall have the best opportunity to get which job. Thus, ethnic groups have clearly emerged as an interest group: an instrumentalist position par excellence. In this connection, one can also refer to Brass (1991), Fenton (1999), Nairn (1977), Rex (1986), Smith (1981) and so on.

Nagel (1995) in a review of resource competition theories that explain the growing ethnicity in terms of competition for resources puts forward three important propositions:

1. Ethnicity is a problematic social category, the boundaries and meaning of which are negotiated by in-group and out-group members.

2. To the extent that resource competition in society is organized along ethnic (rather than class, gender, age, etc.) lines, it has:
   a. increased competition (increases the likelihood of)
   b. ethnic identification (strengthened ethnic boundaries)
   c. racism and prejudice (discrimination and hatred)
   d. inter-ethnic conflict (international and inter-group violence)
   e. ethnic mobilization (movements and collective action).

3. Increased inter-ethnic contact (integration) in the presence of ethnic resource competition increases the likelihood of:
   a. ethnic identification
   b. racism and prejudice
   c. inter-ethnic conflict
   d. ethnic mobilization.

Then he proceeds to enumerate both historical factors such as cultural division of labour, spilt labour market and so on and contemporary factors such as struggle for access to political office and control over political policies that are responsible for ethnic competition resulting in a heightened sense of ethnicity. The point to be remembered is that such factors are present in all the societies, both modern and the so-called non-modern societies. To give one example, affirmative action policies are followed both in India and USA. In both countries, political policies are used to provide some reparation for historically exploited and disadvantaged groups, untouchables in India and the African-Americans in the USA. In both countries, these affirmative action policies promoted ethnic mobilization among the other non-designated minorities who wished to receive similar treatment: religious and linguistic minorities in India and Latin Native Americans and Asian Americans in the United States (Darnell and Parikh 1988, Lopez and Espiritu 1990). In both countries, these political reparation policies promoted a backlash movement by the dominant majority – upper-caste Hindus in India and Whites in the United States (Burstein 1991, Desai 1992). One conclusion that emerges from his essay is that ethnicity in the modern world remains a dynamic and viable basis for acquiring home rule or obtaining favourable political policies within the existing nation-state.

A variant of the instrumental position is the rational-choice theory (Banton 1983). The rational-choice theory, in its application to racial and ethnic relations and probably in most sociological applications, rests on four presuppositions (Banton 1983, p. 479). First, individuals act so as to obtain maximum net advantages. Second, action at one moment in time influences and modifies the alternatives between which individuals will have to choose at subsequent moments. Third, socialization causes humans to recognize their dependence on others and the need to forge selfish gratification at times. Humans can develop their potential only if they are brought up in social groups. Fourth, to attain their ends, individuals will at times be obliged to join with others in collective action. The theory proposed by Banton can be used to explain, for example, the persistence of ethnic identities that will help them gain maximum advantage.

In this context, one can also refer to the optional-situational perspective on ethnicity whose philosophical roots can be traced to symbolic interactionism. The main argument put forward by those subscribing to the optional-situational perspective is that ethnicity can and within certain limits be assumed or put aside by conscious choice (Gleason quoted in Lal 1995, p. 434). The optional-situational perspective sees ethnic identity as a process 'continuously created and recreated adopted and shed, according to the requirements of different social situations' (Peter Berger quoted in Lal 1995, p. 434).

The emphasis on choice and context is reiterated in the American sociologist William Petersen's (1974) contention, 'The ethnic group only exists where members consider themselves to belong to such a group: a conscious sense of belonging is critical' (p. 309). The optional-situational concept of identity can, as Patterson suggests in his essay, accommodate the phenomenon of 'ethnicity by consent'.

This perspective draws our attention to why and how identities do or do not get constructed in situations of varying degrees of constraint. As Ballard and Kalra succinctly observed,

> Exclusion constraints, that is what is all about. What is too often forgotten, however, is that no matter what their focus – be it descent, physical appearance, nationality, gender, occupational, age, caste or whatever – our human capacity to resist these forces is not only immense, but it tends to increase as conditions become ever more severe. Hence behaviour is never wholly determined by forces that constraint it, such that people become helpless pawns, wholly unable to negotiate the terms of their own existence. (1994, p. 485)

What is really important to understand about this perspective is that it conceives of construction of ethnic identities as an ongoing process in which individuals or groups see themselves and define themselves with respect to others in many different ways. From this perspective, ethnicity is an ongoing process and it would not decline. Its form may change, however, depending on the situation.

This approach is preferred by some for essentially four reasons. First, because it is grounded in a subjectivist sociological framework that takes into account the points of view of the actor rather than relying on the sense that the sociologist makes of the actor's world; the optional-situational approach is less likely to overlook the complexity in the ways in which people see themselves and others, especially in seemingly homogeneous groups. Second, the optional-situational perspective treats the emergence of identities such as Black, mixed race, or ethnicity by consent as normal features of multiethnic societies (Benson 1980, Tizard and Phoenix 1993). Third, it is based on the process of collective definition discussed earlier in the optional-situational approach. Ethnic identity is the ability to anticipate and deal with changes in self-definition and redefinition of others as an instance of emergent meaning and as a usual feature of collective life. Fourth, the optional-situational approach brings into the ambit of discussions an aspect of identity that has almost been eclipsed in the literature during the 1970s and 1980s, namely, 'the significant exit' (Lal 1995, p. 436). It is possible that under certain circumstances, an individual might wish to leave his or her ethnic identity behind to replace it with another or to refuse either the support or the disabilities conferred by such an identity. For example, Dalits have tried to escape from the punishing features of casteism through conversion to Buddhism. Modern urban societies, unlike many traditional rural societies, have offered opportunities for individual and groups to effect 'significant exits'.

There have been some attempts to transcend the primordialist-instrumentalist dichotomy. Prominent among them is the oppositional approach suggested by Edward Spicer (1971). The oppositional approach is supposed to provide the basis for the unification of primordial and instrumental positions. According to it neither the primordialist approach nor the instrumentalist approach alone would satisfactorily explain the persistence of ethnicity. He makes use of two central concepts: the persistent identity system and the oppositional process. The oppositional process or the situation of conflict between groups over resources both structural and cultural leads to consolidation of ethnic sentiments and this in turn leads to a high degree of internal solidarity. In the absence of oppositional process, persistent identity systems fail to develop. He cites as an example the Jews, Basque, Irish, Welsh and so on who faced constant pressures for economic, political or religious assimilation into the larger societies and successfully resisted those pressures. By applying this model, one can gain a better understanding of the situation that prevailed in Northern Ireland, Lebanon, Sri Lanka and the then Soviet Union.

In this chapter, my attempt has been to bring various perspectives that deal with the relationship between modernization and ethnicity, either directly or by implication together in order to be able to make sense of the vast literature available on this topic. As would be clear to the readers, I have tried to examine only some of the representative studies, giving references of others wherever necessary. Those who are interested in this area would hopefully find the present attempt a meaningful one.

REFERENCES

Balibar, E. & Wallerstein, I. 1991. *Race, Nation, Class: Ambiguous Identities*. London: Verso.

Ballard, R. & Kalra, V. S. 1994. *The Ethnic Dimensions of the 1991 Census*. Manchester, UK: University of Manchester.

Banks, M. 1996. *Ethnicity: Anthropological Constructions*. London: Routledge.

Banton, M. 1983. *Racial and Ethnic Competition*. Cambridge, UK: Cambridge University Press.

Barth, F. (ed.). 1969. *Ethnic Groups and Boundaries: The Social Organisation of Culture Difference. London*: Allen and Unwin.

Bell, D. 1975. Ethnicity and social change. In N. Glazer & D. Moynihan (eds), *Ethnicity: Theory and Experience* (pp. 141–174). Cambridge, UK: Cambridge University Press.

Benson, S. 1980. *Ambiguous Ethnicity: Interracial Families in London*. Cambridge, UK: Cambridge University Press.

Brass, P. 1991. *Ethnicity and Nationalism: Theory and Comparison*. New Delhi: Sage.

Bromley, Y. 1974. The term ethnos and its definition. In Y. Bromley (ed.), *Soviet Ethnology and Anthropology Today* (pp. 56–72). The Hague: Manton.

Burstein, P. 1991. Reverse discrimination cases in the Federal Courts: Mobilisation by a counter movement. *Sociological Quarterly*, 32(4), 511–528.

Cohen, A. 1969. *Custom and Politics in Urban Africa: A Study of Hausa Migrants in Yoruba Towns*. London: Routledge.

Darnell, A. K. & Parikh, S. 1988. Religion, ethnicity and the role of the state: Explaining conflict in Assam. *Ethnic and Racial Studies*, 11(4), 263–281.

Desai, M. 1992. The demise of secularism and the rise of majority communalism in India. Paper presented at the Annual Meeting of the Midwest Sociological Society, Kansas City, Kansas.

Deutsch, K. W. 1953. *Nationalism and Social Communication*. New York: John Wiley.

Diamond, L. & Plattner, M. F. (eds). 1994. *Nationalism, Ethnic Conflict and Democracy*. Baltimore, MD: Johns Hopkins University Press.

Epstein, A. L. 1958. *Politics in an Urban African Community*. Manchester, UK: Manchester University Press.

Fenton, S. 1999. *Ethnicity: Race, Class and Culture*. London: Macmillan.

Gordon, M. M. 1975. Towards a general theory of racial and ethnic groups relation. In N. Glazer & D. P. Moynihaan (eds), *Ethnicity: Theory and Experience* (pp. 84–110). London: Oxford University Press.

Geertz, P. 1973. *The Interpretation of Cultures*. New York: Basic Books.

Gilroy, P. 1987. *There Ain't No Black in the Union Jack*. London: Hutchison.

Glazer, N. & Moynihan, D. P. 1970. *Beyond the Melting Pot: The Negroes, Puerto Ricans, Jews, Italians and Irish of New York City*. Cambridge, MA: MIT Press.

———. 1975. *Ethnicity: Theory and Experience*. Cambridge, MA: Harvard University Press.

Isaacs, H. 1975. Basic group identity: The ideals of the tribe. In N. Glazer & D. P. Moynihan (eds), *Ethnicity: Theory and Experience* (pp. 29–52). Cambridge, MA: Harvard University Press.

Kupchan, A. (ed.). 1995. *Nationalism and Nationalities in the New Europe*. New York: Cornell University Press.

Lal, B. B. 1995. Symbolic interaction theories. *American Behavioral Scientist*, 38(3), 421–441.

Lopez, D. & Espiritu, Y. 1990. Pan-ethnicity in the United States: A theoretical framework. *Ethnic and Racial Studies*, 13(3), 198–224.

Miles, R. 1984. Marxism versus the sociology of race relations? *Ethnic and Racial Studies*, 6(5), 217–237.

Nagel, J. 1995. Resource competition theories. *American Behavioural Scientist*, 38(3), 442–458.

Nairn, T. 1977. *The Break-up of Britain: Crisis and Neo-nationalism*. London: New Left Books.

Parming, T. & Cheung, L. M. 1980. Modernisation and ethnicity. In J. Dofing & A. Akiwowo (eds.), *National and Ethnic Movements* (pp. 154–162). London: Sage.

Petersen, W. 1974. On the sub nation of Western Europe. In G. Nathan & D. P. Moynihan (eds.), *Ethnicity: Theory and Experience* (pp. 177–208). Cambridge, MA: Harvard University Press.

Rex, J. 1986. *Race and Ethnicity*. Milton Keynes, UK: Open University Press.

Shils, E. 1957. Primordial, personal, sacred and civil ties. In E. Shils (ed.), *Centre and Periphery: Essays in Macro Sociology* (pp. 103–122). Chicago: Chicago University Press.

Smith, A. D. 1981. *The Ethnic Revival*. Cambridge, UK: Cambridge University Press.

Solomos, J. & Back, L. 1995. Marxism, racism and ethnicity. *American Behavioral Scientist*, 38(3), 407–420.

Spicer, E. 1971. Persistent identity systems. *Science*, 411(5), 795–800.

Stack, J. F., Jr. 1986. Ethnic mobilization in world politics: The primordial perspective. In J. F. Stack Jr, *The Primordial Challenge: Ethnicity in the Contemporary World* (pp. 87–93). New York: Greenwood Press.

Tambs-Lynche, H. 1980. *Patidars: A Case Study in Urban Ethnicity*. London: Routledge and Kegan Paul.

Tiryakan, E. A. 1971. The principles of 1789 and sociology. In E. A. Tiryakan (ed.), *The Phenomenon of Sociology* (pp. 45–62). New York: Appleton Century Crafts.

Tishkov, V. 1997. *Ethnicity, Nationalism and Conflict in and after the Soviet Union: The Mind Aflame*. London: Sage.

Tizard, B. & Phoenix, A. 1993. *Black, White or Mixed Race*. London: Sage.

4

Ethnicity, nationalism and modernity

Exploring the linkages

Ethnicity and nationalism have become quite salient in the recent past in the context of the deepening process of modernization (modernity in action). What modernity has done, as we shall see, is that it has changed the ***nature*** and ***character*** of inter-ethnic cultural differences and made them assume the shape of ethnicity and nationalism. It is not that intercultural differences were absent in pre-modern times. They were very much present then. Whatever conflicts that occurred in pre-modern times were not viewed as mainly ethnic conflict between different rulers, tribes, pastoral and sedentary people, and popular uprisings against tyrannical rule were explained in exclusively non-ethnic terms. Although there were revolts by ethnically different enslaved masses, they did not proclaim any sovereign rights based on their ethnic identity; instead, they merely demanded more humane treatment. This has changed now. In our contemporary world system, it has been increasingly observed that ethnic and nationalist conflicts have become a major force. One only had to look around to see the enhanced salience of ethnic and nationalist conflicts. Conflicts between Catholics and Protestants in Northern Ireland; conflicts between the Croats, Serbs and Muslims in Bosnia; massive genocide in Rwanda; and, closer home, the continuing tension manifesting itself in conflicts of different kinds in Kashmir, all of these point to the perpetual salience of ethnicity and nationalism. Nationalism and ethnicity continue to remain key phenomena with which one makes sense of what is happening around us. One of the ugly ways in which nationalism gained scholarly attention in the early 1990s was the Serbian program of 'ethnic cleansing'. Serbs who had earlier allied themselves with the vision of a multiethnic democratic Bosnia and Herzegovina resorted to invocation of ethnic solidarities in the face of civil war and demanded that the Serbs as a whole should be willing to both kill and die for the nation. The events in Yugoslavia were a sufficient indicator of the continued salience of nationalism and ethnicity. Neither ethnic conflicts nor the discourse of national identity nor the practical power of nationalist mobilization has seceded into the pre-modern past despite the confidence of many earlier social scientists (see Debray 1977, Nairn 1975, 1977, Schwarzmantel 1991). We need to understand why this is so and how modernity has become a major factor in explaining away such conflicts.

What is modernity, how does one engage with it and, finally, whether Europe should be considered the only home of modernity are questions that have been dealt with elsewhere (Kumar 2008, 2013). I would therefore refrain from elaborating on it again. Before I proceed further, some conceptual clarification may be in order about the two categorical notions we are concerned with – *ethnicity* and *nationalism* (and by implication *nation*). Ethnicity refers to the *consciousness* of *ethnic identity*. De Vos and Rose define it as 'subjective, symbolic or emblematic use by a group of people . . . of any aspect of culture in order to differentiate themselves from other groups' (1975, p. 16). As Brass said, what is ethnicity to ethnic category is what class consciousness is to class. As far as *nationalism* is concerned, Smith offers us a good starting point in this connection. He defined nationalism as 'an ideological movement for the attainment and maintenance of self-government and independence on behalf of a group, some of whose members conceive it to constitute an actual or potential "nation"' (Smith 1983, p. 171). It is tempting to explain national identities as a transformation of ethnic or cultural similarities wrought by state-building. However, there is a crucial difference between them. Nations are primarily and intrinsically political communities and are sources of sovereignty; however, this is not central to the definition of ethnicities. Nationalism need not simply be seen as a claim of ethnic similarity but as a claim that certain *similarities* should *count* in *the definition* of a *political community*. For this reason, nationalism needs boundaries in a way ethnicity does not. Nationalism demands internal homogeneity throughout a putative nation rather than recognizing the presence of, or need for, gradual continua of cultural variation or pockets of sub-cultural destinations within a sovereign entity or a nation. Perhaps most distinctively, nationalists usually claim that national identities overpower other personal or group identities (such as gender, family or ethnicity) and link individuals directly to the nation as a whole. This is sharply contrary to the way in which most ethnic identities flow from family membership, kinship and membership in intermediate groups. Nations, in short, involve a distinctive new form of group identity or membership. This depends on the new forms of collective imagination and also on communicative capacities and social-organizational conditions that encourage a sense of identity with large population of distant and largely anonymous others. It also depends crucially on modern ideas of individual equivalence.

Modernity of nationalism

The discourse on nationalism is distinctively modern, not before the seventeenth century at the most. In the early modern era the idea of nation as an aggregate of people linked by co-residence or common sociocultural characteristics took political and cultural connotation in struggles with and between states and over state-building. This led to the distinctively modern invocation of nationalism as 'a theory of political legitimacy, which requires that ethnic boundaries should not cut across political ones and in particular, that ethnic boundaries with a given state – a contingency already excluded by the principle in its general formulation – should not separate the power-holders from the rest' (Gellner 1983, p. 1). As Kedourie sums up neatly, 'that humanity is naturally divided into nations, that nations are known by certain characteristics which can be ascertained and that the only legitimate type of government is national self-government' (1960, p. 9). It may also be mentioned here that the modern notion of individualism is embedded in the categories of ethnic group and nation. Earlier in pre-modern times, people were essentially seen as members of social groups by virtue of their occupation and, thus, of a variety of ascribed statuses based on descent, kinship, age and so on. The modern role of self as individual changed this. Personal identity can be increasingly seen as the attribute of a self-contained individual, what Taylor (1989) called as the 'punctual self'. As Schwarcz wrote about protagonists in China's largely nationalistic New Culture movement, 'the alternative to playing the role of so-and-so's son, so- and so's mother etc. is to gain a positive sense of one's own individuality' (1986, p. 112). Such thinkers made it common to understand social groups (including nations and ethnic groups) as sets of equivalent persons rather than as complex webs of relationships and persons positioned within the social hierarchy. Let us take ethnic group as an illustration. Ekeh (1990) noted that there has been a tendency to replace the term *tribe* with the term *ethnic group* in the description of countries in Africa. However, this has the effect of imposing a categorical definition that a nation is but a collection of individuals marked by common ethnicity in place of a definition that puts emphasis on relational links between people within a sovereign country. Whereas the notion of tribe pointed to the centrality of kinships, the notion of ethnic group implies that a detailed, serious analysis of kinship is more or less irrelevant. Barth (1969) took this a step further and abandoned even the notion of subjective belief in common descent, replacing it with simply the existence of recognized group boundaries. Here the categorical logic achieves complete supremacy. An ethnic group is simply a bounded set of individuals, not necessarily characterized by any internal pattern of relationships, much less one of kinship order. Once ethnic groups are treated in this purely categorical way – as they are in everyday contemporary discourse as well as in academic studies – similarities rather than relationships form the definite connection among members. This opens the doors for new members to conform to such categorization.

Apart from this, nations are genuinely seen as logical equivalents and, thus, individuals. In Meinecke's words (1970, p. 89), 'Nations are individualities with particular talents and the possibility of exploiting those talents.' Anderson has seized on this aspect of individuality as central to the modern understanding of nation. In his own words, 'The idea of sociological organism moving calendrically through homogeneous, empty time is a precise analogue of the idea of the nation, while it is also conceived as a solid community moving steadily down (or up) history' (1991, p. 26). As stressed by Anderson, the category of nation unites the living and the dead. This is a crucial explanation for why the nation can demand such extraordinary sacrifices and commitments from its members. It joins the biographies of individual persons and of the nation as a whole in a common historical narrative. Not only does the nation locate individual temporarily in relation to past and future generations and in the global context as members of one among many nations, it also locates each individual biography as one among the many comparable biographies of the members of the specific nation.

The rise of imperialism, industrialization, urbanization, migration and deepened process of democratization are all viewed as essentially modern processes that have contributed in their own way to the sharpening-up of ethnic and nationalist consciousness. Imperialism is inextricably connected with the project of modernity, and its decline has been considered as a positive thing. However, it must be remembered that the end of imperialism has left many states in a highly disturbed state of affairs. Sharper hostility between ethnic nations and weak states is one of the most conspicuously negative consequences of modernity. The Industrial Revolution and rise of modern empires have led to massive migration of people looking for job opportunities and/or safer places to live away from oppression in their own 'home' states. As a result inter-ethnic interaction has increased substantially, leading at times to increased friction between different ethnic groups. The groups whose expectations and hopes have not been fulfilled have sought to structure their language of frustration in ethnic and nationalist terms. In the wake of communism's collapse, nationalism and ethnic conflict became the primary issues in the realignment of Eastern European politics and identity. Appeals to the idea of nation resonated across continents, for example, from organized movements of ethnic separation from Quebec (Birch 1989, Taylor 1992) to the postcolonial states of Africa (Davidson 1992). New nationalisms proliferated through the developed West (Smith 1981), and attempts were made to decolonize the discourse of nationalism in the Third World and drive it to bolster indigenous movements and meanings (Blaut 1987, Chatterjee 1986). There is a strong view that sees not only nationalism but also nationhood as basically following from, rather than shaping, the rise of European modernity. Nations are in this view produced by the rise of states and/or the capitalist world system. As Giddens puts it, 'By a "nation," I refer to a collectivity existing within a clearly demarcated territory, which is subject to a unitary administration, reflexively monitored both by the internal state apparatus and those of other state. A nation as I use the term here only exists when a state has a unified administrative reach over the territory over which its sovereignty is claimed' (1984, p. 116). In his understanding, the relationship between nationalism and ethnicity is more or less coincidental. It is the modern state that defines nationhood, and pre-existing ethnic relations are revised either to coincide more or less with its boundaries to constitute the basis of counter-state movement mobilized for the formation of a new state. Such movements are rooted in power relations, not in ethnic solidarities.

Nationalisms, it must also be mentioned, vary between claims that consider traditional identity such as ethnicity superfluous in the context of the founding of a free and modern nation and claims to national identity and sovereignty rooted precisely in ancient ethnicity. An example of this paradigmatic contrast between these two forms of nationalism can be seen in the nationalism literature focusing on the development of nationalisms in France and Germany. In both cases historical narratives are mobilized to underpin the nationalist myth. The French narrative traces the nation to a modern act of founding by its members, some of whom were not 'French' proper, until the galvanization of radically novel nation-founding movement that gave rise to the French Republic.

It emphasizes the view that nation-making involves necessarily conversion of a group of people with common identity, 'the French' in this case, into a political form such as the republic and, thus, giving recognition and legitimacy to the idea of 'French' citizenship (Beet 1988). In contrast, the German nationalist history writing pushes further back in pursuit of a 'naturalizing' account of German ethnicity; that is, Germany must be rooted in an 'always already existing' ethnic identity. German nationalists, from Herder to Fichte, have emphasized on 'ethnic' rather than 'political' or 'civic' as a criteria or pre-condition for inclusion in nation-building (see Alter 1989, Kedourie 1960, 1974). When Renan (1990) described the nation as a 'daily plebiscite' he was not making a universalizing statement or offering a definition. He was distinguishing those nations (such as France) that were the result of the free choices of their members from those (such as Germany) whose identity and cohesion are given to their members independently of any voluntary will. Such differences in nationalist narratives have practical consequences. Since voluntary will is so crucial to the narrative of French nationalism France makes it easier for immigrants to attain its citizenship compared to Germany.

Nationalism and the modern economic process

Nationalism has come to be closely identified with massive modern economic changes that have characterized the West to begin with and later spread to all parts of the world. It has been argued that one cannot look at nationalism in isolation from the modern processes that are currently underway (Kumar 2010). According to Gellner, nationalism is inextricably connected to modernity. Although there was a pre-existing ethnicity, it cannot adequately explain the renewed salience of nationalism in the modern period. He is of the view that the understanding of nation and nationalism and their birth and growth has become so powerful and dominant that one cannot remain indifferent to it. The most essential point he makes about nationalism is that it is nationalism that leads to nations rather than the other way around. Nations emerge out of the ideology of nationalism. Nationalism invents nations where they already do not exist. This begs the question, how does nationalism emerge? And before that we need to consider another question, what is nationalism, according to Gellner? One cannot help but quote him at length on the definition of nationalism. In his own words,

> Nationalism is the general imposition of a high culture on society, where previously low had taken up the lives of the majority and in some cases the totality of the population. It means the general diffusion of a school-mediated, academy-supervised idiom, codified for the requirements of a reasonably precise bureaucratic and technological communication. It is the establishment of an anonymous impersonal society, with mutually substitutable atomised individuals, held together above all by a shared culture of this kind, in place of the previous complex structure of local groups, sustained by folk cultures reproduced locally and idiosyncratically by the micro-groups themselves. (Gellner 1983, p. 57)

Gellner looks at the birth of nationalism in terms of both positive social foundations and, for want of a better term, what can be called negative social foundations. Positively, nationalism is a product of the process of industrialization. This process requires the development of highly advanced forms of communication, as the work to be done is mostly semantic, which in turn requires development of standardized means of communication, that is, development of a uniform language. A uniform language generates greater cultural identification. According to Gellner, 'Modern people do not in general become nationalists from sentiments or sentimentality atavistic or not, well-based or myth-founded: they become nationalists, through genuine, objective, practical necessity, however obscurely recognized' (Gellner 1964, p. 160). Its evolution can be mapped as follows: Industrialization → nationalism → nation.

Such a way of looking at the emergence of nationalism is explicitly functionalist in nature. Gellner's theory of nationalism is credited with having almost reified functionalism. In fact, Perry Anderson, grandfather of the Marxist New Left, argues that the 'most arresting feature of Gellnerian theory of nationalism is its single-minded economic functionalism' (1992, p. 207). One could go directly to Gellner and indicate the functionalist cast of his argument in his own words: 'So the economy needs both the new type of central culture and the central State; the culture needs the State and the State probably needs the homogenous cultural branding of its flock. . . . In brief, the mutual relationship of a modern culture and State is something quite new and springs, inevitably, from the requirement of a modern economy' (1983, p. 48). If one takes this proposition to its logical conclusion, they can arrive at five important formulations (Elster 1983, p. 135):

(i) Nationalism is inevitably an effect of modernization.

(ii) Nationalism is beneficial for modernizing states because a highly specialized division of labour requires a unified high culture that is underpinned by a highly developed and specialized educational system.

(iii) Nationalism (in Gellnerian sense) is unintended by the actors producing modernization.

(iv) The causal relationship between nationalism and modernization is not recognized by the agents operating in modernizing societies.

(v) Nationalism functionally maintains modernization by a feedback loop operating through the action of modernizing states.

Negatively, the uneven spread of modernization has a huge potential in generating nationalist aspirations. Uneven modernization aggravates the existing inequalities among differently placed groups, and the intelligentsia from the deprived groups harp on their separate distinctive identity as a means, a weapon in their hands, for overcoming the structures of inequality. The result is the birth of nationalist movements. In Gellner's own words, 'Nationalism is not the awakening of nations to self-consciousness: it invents nations where they do not exist but it does need some pre-existing differentiating marks to work on, even if ... these are purely negative' (1964, p. 168).

It is now a part of his philosophy of history that looks at three important phases in human societies: (i) pre-agrarian, (ii) agrarian and (iii) industrial. In the pre-agrarian societies it would be senseless to talk of nationalism as they were essentially stateless societies, and speaking about them in the context of a formal nation-state would be meaningless. In the agrarian societies the elites did not share a common culture with masses, and, in the absence of a common culture, nationalist ideology would have had no basis. The industrial society, on the other hand, needs to have a proper communication among its people, which would mean that there has to be a common language to facilitate such a communication.

A nation is, in Anderson's (1991) evocative phrase, an 'imagined community'. He suggests that we regard nationalism as a distinct mode of understanding and constituting the phenomenon of belonging together, comparable to kinship or religion. A nation, thus, 'is an imagined political community. It is imagined because the members of even the smallest nation will never know most of their fellow-members, meet them or even hear of them, yet in the mind of each lives the image of their communion' (1991, pp. 6–7). The nation is imagined as linked because even the largest of them, encompassing perhaps a billion living human beings, has finite, if elastic boundaries, beyond which lie other nations. It is imagined as sovereign because the concept was born in an age in which Enlightenment and Revolution were destroying the legitimacy of the divinely ordained, hierarchical dynastic realm. Finally, it is imagined as a community because regardless of the actual inequality and exploitation that may prevail in each, the nation is always conceived as a deep horizontal comradeship.

In the context of nationalism, Anderson offers three main arguments: (i) language is essentially a cultural condition of nationalism. Nationalist imaginings took place through a language. By looking for ever-larger markets, capitalist cultural production (in the form of books and newspapers, a distinctly modern process) called forth 'unified fields of exchange and communication below Latin and above the spoken vernaculars' (1991, p. 44). That is, in early modern Europe capitalism sought markets larger than the small number of elite readers of Latin and larger than the number of speakers of nearly all local vernaculars. Thus, they pioneered the creation of specific linguistic communities associated with eventual national ideologies. (ii) After talking about the role of language in the creation of ethnic foundations for nationalism, Anderson's formulation of 'print capitalism' also helped to make sense of the new kind of imagining of community more directly. The readers of the same novels and newspapers were joined in imagining communities of other such readers and of imagining commonality with the protagonists of the stories they read (1991, pp. 24–36). The readers of daily newspapers learned not only the same news as each other, they also learned 'wholly new ideas of simultaneity' (1991, p. 37). They learned to situate themselves in terms of the activities of many individuals (and nation) taking place in the same temporal moment, not solely in a linear development. This also allowed for a sense of shared paths, which could arise historically only when substantial groups of people were in a position to think of themselves as living lives parallel to those of other groups of people – if never meeting yet certainly proceeding along the same trajectory. (iii) The importance of communication media to nation integration has certainly been noted before (see Deutsch 1953). In most earlier treatments, the categorical identity of the nation has been preserved, and research focused on how the development of communication capacities enhanced the social and political integration of the nation. Anderson's central contribution is to explain how communicative forms figured in creating the categorical identity or imagined community of the nation itself.

Against this backdrop, however, one also needs to be aware of alternative voices. Anthony Smith (1983, 1986 and 1991) argues that nationalism has stronger roots in pre-modern ethnicity. Nations are rooted in relatively ancient histories, though he admits that nationalism, as ideology and movement, dates only from the eighteenth century. Nevertheless, Smith says that ethnic origins of nations are much older. He argues that 'myths, symbols, memories and values are "carried" in and by artifacts and activities which change only very slowly, so ethnic, once formed, tend to be exceptionally durable under "normal" vicissitudes and to persist over many generations, even centuries forming "moulds" within which all kinds of social and cultural processes can unfold and upon which all kinds of circumstances and pressures can exert an impact' (1986, p. 16). Rooted in ethnicity, nations are long-term processes, continually re-enacted and reconstructed; they require ethnic cores, homelands, heroes and golden ages if they are to survive. Small, breakaway nations rooted in particularist quasi-religious visions are the most common new nationalist projects today. Thus, Smith says, 'Modern nations and nationalism have only extended and deepened the meanings and scope of older ethnic concepts and structures. Nationalism has certainly universalised these structures and ideals, but modern "civic" nations have not in practice really transcended ethnicity or ethnic sentiment' (1986, p. 216).

Smith does not claim that ethnicity is natural but views it as socially constructed. His argument is that ethnicity is very slow to change. He acknowledges also that pre-modern ethnic boundaries were not sharply fixed, though he does claim that they maintained a level of integrity. Above all, Smith suggests that it is possible to trace 'genealogy of nations' in which both cultural and social structural variables can be introduced to account for which ethnies become nations. The crucial moment in such genealogies, he suggests, is the transformation of the members of an ethnie into citizens. This is a cultural transformation of the character of membership, stressing the lateral ties that link members despite class divisions and that form the basis for potential political mobilization (Smith 1986, p. 166). The important point to be remembered is that he stressed continuity in ethnic groupings and the relation of cultural similarity that defines them.

Conclusion

The relationship between nationalism, ethnicity and modernity is highly complex. Both nationalism and ethnicity are very much part of a modern set of categorical identities invoked by elites and other participants in political and social struggles. These categorical identities also shape everyday life offering both tools for grasping pre-existing homogeneity and difference and constructing specific versions of such identity. Numerous dimensions of modern social and cultural change, notably state-building, individualism and the integration of large-scale webs of indirect relationship, all serve to make both nationalism and ethnicity salient. Nationalism, in particular, remains the preeminent rhetoric for attempting to demarcate political community's claim to right of self-determination and legitimate rule by reference to 'the people' of a country in the modern era. Ethnic solidarities and identities are claimed most often where groups do not seek 'national' autonomy but recognition of internal, or cross-cutting, national or state boundaries. The essential point that emerges from the above discussion is that nationalism and ethnicity are organically connected to the project of modernity.

REFERENCES

Alter, P. 1989. *Nationalism*. London: Arnold.

Anderson, B. 1991. *Imagined Communities: Reflections on the Origin and Spread of Nationalism*. London: Verso.

Anderson, P. 1992. Science, politics and enchantment. In J. A. Hall & I. C. Jarvie (eds), *Transitions to Modernity: Essays on Power, Wealth and Belief* (pp. 202–232). Cambridge, UK: Cambridge University Press.

Barth, F. (ed.). 1969. *Ethnic Boundaries*. Oslo, Norway: Norwegian University Press.

Beet, G. (ed.). 1988. *The Permanent Revolution: The French Revolution and Its Legacy*. Chicago: Chicago University Press.

Birch, A. H. 1989. *Nationalism and National Integration*. London: Allen & Unwin.

Blaut, J. 1987. *The National Question: Decolonising the Theory of Nationalism*. Atlantic Highlands, NJ: Zed Books.

Chatterjee, P. 1986. *Nationalist Thought and the Colonial World: A Derivative Discourse*. Atlantic Highlands, NJ: Zed Books.

Davidson, B. 1992. *The Black Man's Burden: Africa and the Curse of the Nation-state*. Cambridge, UK: Cambridge University Press.

Debray, R. 1977. Marxism and the national question. *New Left Review,* 105, 20–41.

Deutsch, K. W. 1953. *Nationalism and Social Communication: An Inquiry into the Foundations of Nationality*. Cambridge, MA: MIT Press.

————. 1969. *Nationalism and Its Alternatives*. New York: Alfred A Knopf.

De Vos, G. & Rose, L. R. (eds). 1975. *Ethnic Identity: Cultural Continuity and Change*. Mayfield: Palo Allow.

Ekeh, P. R. 1990. Social anthropology and two contrasting uses of tribalism in Africa. *Comparative Study of Social History*, 32(4), 660–700.

Elster, J. 1983. *Explaining Technical Change*. Cambridge, UK: Cambridge University Press.

Gellner, E. 1964. *Thought and Change*. London: Weidenfeld and Nicolson.

———. 1983. *Nation and Nationalism*. Ithaca, NY: Cornell University Press.

Giddens, A. 1984. *The Nation-State and Violence*. Berkeley, CA: University of California Press.

Kedourie, E. 1960. *Nationalism*. Westport, CT: Praeger.

———. 1974. *Nationalism in Asia and Africa*. New York: New American Library.

Kohn, H. 1967. *The Idea of Nationalism*. New York: Collier.

Kumar, D. V. 2008. Engaging with modernity: Need for a critical negotiation. *Sociological Bulletin,* 57(2), 240–254.

————. 2010. Gellnerian theory of nation and nationalism: A critical appraisal. *Sociological Bulletin,* 59(3), 392–406.

————. 2013. Contesting the European origins of modernity. *The Eastern Anthropologist,* 66(4), 437–448.

Meinecke, F. 1970. *Cosmopolitism and the National State*. Princeton, NJ: Princeton University press.

Nairn, T. 1975. The modern Janus. *New Left Review*, 94, 3–30.

Nairn, T. 1977. *The Break-up of Britain: Crisis and Neo-nationalism*. London: New Left Books.

Renan, E. 1990. What is a nation? In H. Bhabha (ed.), *Nation and Narrative* (pp. 8–22). London: Routledge.

Schwarcz, V. 1986. *The Chinese Enlightenment. Intellectuals and the Legacy of the May Fourth Movement of 1919*. Berkeley, CA: University of California Press.

Schwarzmantel, J. 1991. *Socialism and the Idea of the Nation*. Hemel Hempstead, UK: Harvester Wheatsheaf.

Seton-Watson, H. 1977. *Nations and States*. Boulder, CO: Westview.

Smith, A. D. 1981. *The Ethnic Revival in the Modern World*. Cambridge, UK: Cambridge University press.

———. 1983. *Theories of Nationalism*. London: Duckworth.

———. 1986. *The Ethnic Origin of Nation*. Oxford, UK: Blackwell.
———. 1991. *National Identity*. London: Penguin.
Taylor, C. 1989. *The Sources of Self-Knowledge*. Harvard, MA: Harvard University Press.
———. 1992. *The Politics of Recognition*. Princeton, NJ: Princeton University Press.

5

Gellnerian theory of nation and nationalism

A critical appraisal

Nationalism continues to evoke great passion. The enormous power it wields even in the context of globalization and 'high modernity' would make it necessary to take a critical relook at its formulation, which has found wide acceptability both among scholars and laymen; some scholars argue that nationalist consciousness would gradually weaken as changes of profound nature occur. The confident assertion made by Horsman and Marshall that 'the advanced industrial societies only hold up a mirror to the future of the planet, when nations and nationalism will be revealed as transient forces which are fast becoming obsolete in a world of vast transnational markets, power blocks, global consumerism and mass communications' (1994, p. 102) needs to be taken with a pinch of salt. The power that nationalism demonstrates now and then continues to demand our continual engagement with it in terms of understanding why and how it remains a dominant narrative. In this chapter I will pursue such an engagement by making a critical appreciation of

Gellnerian account of the growth of nations and nationalism. I will place Gellnerian account of nation and nationalism within the broad theoretical paradigm of modernism that has immense explanatory power. What I will do in the following pages is that I will briefly look at different variants of modernism that deal with the question of birth and growth of nation and nationalism, then revisit Gellnerian arguments about nationalism examining some of the serious problems they suffer from and finally suggest certain reformulations in his theory that, I think, would make his theory of nationalism more meaningful and satisfactory in terms of making sense of nationalism. Although Gellner was one of those scholars who took the position that nations would eventually dissolve, I am not particularly interested in looking at this aspect of his theory. I am rather interested in looking at his account of the birth and growth of nations and nationalism and how it could be reformulated, given certain weaknesses in his theory, to make it more relevant and meaningful.

At this juncture, a preliminary comment can be made about the nature of nationalism. Nationalism has a dialectical quality about it. It is both inclusionary and exclusionary at the same time. The very process of including people who share the same objective and subjective characteristics in the political community of nation inevitably excludes those who do not share these. There could also be an endless argument as to who should be included and who should be excluded. It is also dialectical in another sense. It can be constructive as well as destructive. Nationalism can have an enormous emancipatory potential in terms of mobilizing oppressed, disadvantaged and deprived groups under the rubric of nationalism and motivating them to struggle for their own social, economic and political betterment. It can also have destructive potential in the sense that nationalism as a sentiment could be used by powerful groups to marginalize and subjugate the weaker ones. Some, however, focus more on the destructive aspects of nationalism. Kedourie, for instance, may regard nationalism as destructive of all political orders, though he himself spent a lot of time trying to understand the birth and growth of nationalism (1998). Whichever way one looks at it, the dialectical nature of nationalism needs to be recognized.

There is a need to have certain familiarity, in a Durkheimian sense, with the concepts we are going to make use of, that is, nation and nationalism, before we try and understand their growth and dynamics. Smith offers us a good starting point in this connection. He defines nationalism as 'an ideological movement for the attainment and maintenance of self-government and independence on behalf of a group, some of whose members conceive it to constitute an actual or potential "nation", (1983, p. 171). It would also be useful to look at the definition of nation offered by him. He defines nation as 'a group of human beings, possessing common and distinctive elements of culture, a unified economic system, citizenship rights for all members, a sentiment of solidarity arising out of common experiences, and occupying a common territory' (1973, p. 18).

Apart from the modernist interpretation of nation and nationalism, which we will be looking at shortly, there are other paradigms that have become influential, at different points of time, as ways of looking at nations and nationalism. Although they too make a serious attempt to understand the growth and the trajectory of nations, they suffer, in my view, from very serious limitations. Perennialism, for example, would like to maintain that nations existed for a long time. It is not hard to sustain such a formulation. By producing 'hard data' and some tangible remains of distant material culture, it should be possible to refer to nation as being a historical reality (Diaz-Andreu and Smith 2001, Kohl and Fawcett 1995). The essential problem with this kind of understanding of nation is that it lacks an explanatory power. It does not enable us to understand why and how nations always existed. Similarly primordialism, another paradigm, looks at nations as having ineffable and affective significance for the members (Geertz 1973, Shils 1957, Van den Berghe 1978, 1979, 1995). A serious limitation with this formulation is that it does not enable us to appreciate the fluctuation in the intensity of expression of ethnic and nationalist aspirations (Kumar 2006, p. 67).

Modernism

Modernism, on the other hand, as a theoretical paradigm, as I look at it, has an immense explanatory power in terms of analysing the growth of nations and nationalism. Modernism in the nationalist literature looks at nations and nationalism as essentially modern in nature. They are a product of modernity. An attempt has been made elsewhere to make sense of what modernity is and elaborate and interrogate different forms of engaging with it (Kumar 2008). We will therefore refrain from pursing it further. As far as the modernist way of looking at nations and nationalism is concerned, it needs to be stated that this has two distinct connotations: chronological and sociological (Smith 2001, p. 46). In the chronological sense it would mean that nation has emerged in the recent past, not earlier than a century or so. Sociologically it indicates that the nature of nationalism is qualitatively novel. It is a product of conditions that are completely new. Nationalism as an ideology or a movement is not an updated version of seeking something that existed before. Its nature and character are completely novel because the conditions that have given rise to it are new and novel.

This paradigm has different variants (Smith 2001, p. 47). These variants differ with one another in terms of looking at the characteristics of different forms of nationalism and conditions that have given rise to nationalism. The *socioeconomic variety* of modernism would look at nations as products of economic forces such as industrial capitalism and their consequences for the society. Because of uneven development of capitalism, certain regions and places continue to remain in a backward state. As a result, groups living in these regions suffer from a sense of relative deprivation that gets ethnicized. Ethnic sentiments get aroused and mobilization of people takes place along ethnic (nationalist) lines (Hechter 1975, Nairn 1977). Fundamentally, it is the economic forces that led to the emergence of ethnic/nationalist movements. However, this approach would leave open the question as to *why* mobilization of people should not take place along different lines, say, class lines. Simply stating that sentiments get ethnicized and mobilization of people would take place along ethnic lines would not suffice. The other is that of *sociocultural type*. From this perspective, nationalisms are seen as a necessary cultural accompaniment to the process of modernization (of which industrialization is the main expression). The process of industrialization demands free communication among people and breakdown of linguistic barriers. In this context, it is stated that schools play a crucial role in producing individuals who have the necessary skills and are able to engage in communication with each other. Sharing of the same language is a crucial attribute of nationalism. Nationalism plays a functional role for the industrial society. It facilitates proper functioning of a modern and industrial society (Gellner 1964, 1983, 1987, 1994, 1996). However, the sociocultural variety of modernism, to which I broadly subscribe, suffers from serious problems that need to be examined critically and subjected to certain reformulations so that it becomes a more relevant and satisfactory theoretical paradigm, which I will attempt to do shortly.

The *political variety* of nationalism may argue that nations and nationalism emerge out of the changing dynamics of the relations between the State and society. Groups and communities that do not wish to be part of any particular State try to secede from that. In this process new nations and nationalism emerge emphasizing the principle of autonomy and sovereignty (Breuilly 1993, Giddens 1985, Mann 1984). Although this approach does take into account the changing dynamics of relations between the State and society, it does not deal adequately with the dynamics of ethnic/nationality formation. What would be the basis of group formation and why one basis and not the other are some of the issues that are not taken up for a serious interrogation. According to the *constructionist paradigm*, which is the fourth variety of modernism, nations are looked at in terms of their socially constructed nature. Among the powerful theorists who take this position are Benedict Anderson (1991) and Eric Hobsbawm (1990). For Anderson nations are imagined political communities. They are imagined because it is impossible for members of a nation to know each other directly. Still they have a strong sense of belonging to a common nation. This sense emerged out of the materials they use to construct nation. Nationalism, according to Eric Hobsbawm, owes much to 'invented traditions' that are products of social engineering and are created to serve the interests of ruling elites by channelling the energies of the newly enfranchised masses. However, his use of term 'invented' (in the sense of being fabricated) is amenable to a sustained critique because this negates the attempts to reconstruct and re-appropriate some of the already existing customs, traditions, myths, memories and symbols that are in consonance with the sentiments and feelings of people for the purpose of mobilizing people. Any project to mobilize people needs to take into account the fact that anything completely 'new' would not strike chord with them and it necessarily has to depend on the already existing cultural resources to be able to successfully mobilize people.

Gellnerian understanding of nationalism

As stated in the beginning, we would be looking critically at Gellnerian's understanding of nations and nationalism and why it needs to be reformulated to make it a more useful and satisfactory theoretical paradigm. His understanding of nation and nationalism, their birth and growth, has become so powerful and dominant that one cannot remain indifferent to it (O'Leary 1998). His ideas on nationalism compel the engagement of all those who are interested in the study of nationalism. His way of looking at nationalism posed a serious challenge to the intellectual hegemony of conservatives who dominated before the Enlightenment and rationalists who began to dominate the intellectual space after the Enlightenment took place in Europe. He rejected religion as a legitimate principle of political order, an idea that was a direct challenge to the conservatives for whom religion constituted the core principle. Against secular rationalists he was arguing that material prosperity, utility, law and so on were of secondary importance in establishing a stable and legitimate political order. This invited strong condemnation from rationalists, liberals and sociologists for some 200 years (Hobsbawm 1990).

The most essential point he makes about nationalism is that it is nationalism that leads to nations rather than the other way around. Nations emerge out of the ideology of nationalism. Nationalism invents nations where they already do not exist. The question comes: how does nationalism emerge, and before that, what is nationalism for Gellner? One cannot but quote him at length on the definition of nationalism. In his own words, 'Nationalism is the general imposition of a high culture on society, where previously low had taken up the lives of the majority and in some cases the totality of the population. It means the general diffusion of a school-mediated, academy-supervised idiom, codified for the requirements of a reasonably precise bureaucratic and technological communication. It is the establishment of an anonymous impersonal society, with mutually substitutable atomized individuals, held together above all by a shared culture of this kind, in place of the previous complex structure local groups, sustained by folk cultures reproduced locally and idiosyncratically by the micro-groups themselves' (Gellner 1983, p. 57).

Gellner looks at the birth of nationalism in terms of both positive social foundations and, for want of a better term, what can be called negative social foundations. Positively, nationalism is a product of the process of industrialization. This process requires the development of highly advanced forms of communication as the work to be done is mostly semantic; which in turn requires development of standardized means of communication, that is, development of a uniform language. A uniform language generates greater cultural identification. In his own words, 'Modern people do not in general become nationalists from sentiments or sentimentality atavistic or not, well-based or myth-founded: they become nationalists, through genuine, objective, practical necessity, however obscurely recognized' (Gellner 1964, p. 160). It could be represented as follows:

Industrialization → nationalism → nation

Such a way of looking at the emergence of nationalism is explicitly functionalist in nature. His theory of nationalism is credited with having almost reified functionalism. In fact, Perry Anderson, grandfather of the Marxist New Left, argues that the 'most arresting feature of Gellnerian theory of nationalism is its single-minded economic functionalism' (1992, p. 207). One could go directly to Gellner and indicate the functionalist cast of his argument in his own words: 'So the economy needs both the new type of central culture and the central State; the culture needs the State and the State probably needs the homogenous cultural branding of its flock. . . . In brief, the mutual relationship of a modern culture and State is something quite new and springs, inevitably, from the requirement of a modern economy' (1983, p. 48). If one takes this proposition to its logical conclusion, one would arrive at the following (Elster 1983, p. 135).

1. Nationalism is an effect of modernization.
2. Nationalism is beneficial for modernizing states, because a highly specialized division of labour requires a unified high culture, which is underpinned by a highly developed and specialized educational system.
3. Nationalism (in Gellnerian sense) is unintended by the actors producing modernization.
4. The causal relationship between nationalism and modernization is not recognized by the agents operating in modernizing societies.
5. Nationalism functionally maintains modernization by a feedback loop operating through the action of modernizing states.

Negatively, the uneven spread of modernization has a huge potential in generating nationalist aspirations. Uneven modernization aggravates the existing inequalities among differently placed groups and the intelligentsia from the deprived groups harp on their separate distinctive identity as a means, a weapon in their hands, for overcoming the structures of inequality. The result is the birth of nationalist movements. In Gellner's own words, 'Nationalism is not the awakening of nations to self-consciousness: it invents nations where they do not exist but it does need some pre-existing differentiating marks to work on, even if ... these are purely negative' (1964, p. 168).

It is now a part of his philosophy of history that looks at three important phases in human societies: (i) pre-agrarian, (ii) agrarian and (iii) industrial. In the pre-agrarian societies it would be senseless to talk of nationalism as they were essentially stateless societies, and, therefore, discussing about their dynamics or social structure in terms of modern nation-states would be meaningless. In the agrarian societies the elites did not share a common culture with masses, and in the absence of a common culture nationalist ideology would have had no basis. The industrial society, on the other hand, needs to have a proper communication among its people, which would mean that there has to be a common language to facilitate such a communication.

Gellner's theory of nationalism, if not properly reformulated, is vulnerable to some serious problems. One of the most important grounds on which his theory could be taken to task is that it is explicitly instrumentalist and functionalist, as mentioned above, in orientation. According to this point of view, Gellner looks at nationalism as being functional for modernization (Anderson 1991, p. 207). Nationalism strengthens the process of modernization and industrialization by harping on high culture. Without a shared high culture (nationalism), modernization would not be successful. Thus, it becomes clear from the above that his explanation is teleological in nature, that is, explaining the causes of a phenomenon in terms of the needs it serves. His idea that the industrial society characterized as it is by social mobility, relative egalitarianism, anonymity, semantic/communicative rather than physical work requires a context-free medium of communication; that is, a nationalist ideology based on mass literacy/education has a functional and teleological slant to it. This understanding leads to the impression, as stated above, that the needs of 'Industria' are illegitimately transformed into causes that more or less automatically create nationalism. Such a position would neglect the active involvement of people in the construction of nationalism. One need not be a hardcore phenomenologist to appreciate the active involvement of people in producing nationalism. Apart from being teleological, its neglect of actors' perspective needs to be seriously questioned.

The second problem that is associated with his theory is that he has ignored the passions, emotions that are deeply implicated in the birth of nationalism. He only looks at it as a product of modernization, thus underpinning its instrumentalist dimension. It must, however, be recognized that nationalism is not something that simply emerges as a matter of natural course from the process of modernization. Rather it is something that requires the investment of considerable energy and time on the part of those who are involved in bringing it about, a point that has not been given sufficient importance by Gellner.

Third, as some would argue, he has also been found to be wrong on his thesis that nationalism is a product of industrialization. Contrary to this idea, it has been argued that nationalism existed before industrialization (Armstrong 1982, Smith 1986). It has also been argued that establishing a kind of causality between the two – industrialism and nationalism – would be problematical in the absence of conclusive proof. In fact, it is possible to think of societies where industrialization has occurred without being accompanied by nationalism or of societies where nationalism happened without industrialization. For example, Mouzalis refers to proto-industrialization of several regions in Western Europe where the former has occurred and the Balkans and Latin America in the nineteenth century where the latter has taken place (1998, p. 158). He would go further and argue, citing scholars such as Mann, Anthony Giddens and others, that nationalism has not happened because of the development of markets and industry, the position taken by Gellner. Rather it was because of the development of the state and its institutions such as military, bureaucracy, advanced forms of tax structure that actually resulted in the destruction of political, economic and cultural localism. The 'infrastructural development of the state', to use Mann's terminology, eventually led to the transformation of absolutist states into nation-states, and of 'subjects' into 'citizens' (Mann 1984).

Fourth, another charge that has been levelled against Gellner is that his account of birth of nationalism is not sufficiently political in nature. It does not take sufficient note of the political dynamics that underlies the nationalist movements. It is too immersed in the materialist foundations of nationalism that it does not have any space for the political nature of nationalism. Arguing along these lines, O' Leary makes an important point that Gellnerian theory appears to rely on materially reductionist accounts of nationalism (1998, p. 63). The kind of role that power-politics plays in determining which cultures become nations has not been dealt with in this theorization.

To be honest to Gellner, he did try and give elaborate answers to his critics (1996). Against the first criticism, for example, he argues that his theory is *not* teleological and that he has attempted to provide a deeply causal account of the growth of nationalism. He has avoided the illegitimate transformation of needs into causes by spelling out the *mechanisms* that link industrial functional requirements with the emergence and consolidation of a literacy-linked, context-free nationalist idiom. These mechanisms are related to the fact the people who are unable to acquire such a nationalist idiom feel enormously disadvantaged and discriminated.

Similarly, reacting to the criticism that he is indifferent to emotions entertained by the people, he argues that he understands the power of nationalism for the people and communities. More precisely, in his own words, 'Nationalism is not explained by the use it has in legitimizing modernization – a view with which I am quite mistakenly credited – but by the fact that individuals find themselves in very stressful situations, unless the nationalist requirement of congruence between a man's culture and that of his environment is satisfied. Hence that deep passion which, according to Perry Anderson, is absent both from my theory and my bosom. As it happens, it is very much present in both of them. The passion is not a means to some end. It is a reaction to an intolerable situation, to a constant jarring in the activity which is by far the most important thing in life – contact and communication with fellow human beings' (1996, pp. 627–628).

Despite his attempt to give elaborate answers to his critics, there is one missing link in his theory that needs to be taken note of. While I am broadly in agreement with the formulation that nationalism (understood as an ideology, movement, sentiment) and nations (defined in terms of common memory, language, claim over a 'homeland', public culture, equal citizenship rights and duties, language, striving for political sovereignty with their own states etc.) are a modern phenomenon and their rise needs to be explained in terms of political and economic conditions that obtain in the modern world, as Gellner sought to do, I would, however, like to argue that their links with ethnies, with their collective identity, memory, myth and sentiments need to be recognized. In other words, I would like to view nations as having been constructed out of ethnic materials. The essential problem that I find with his theory of nationalism is that except for saying that nations need to work on some pre-existing differentiating marks, it does not really elaborate much on this very crucial point. This is where there is a strong need to recognize the ethnic roots of nations.

At this juncture, a little clarification is required. It should be clear that the formulation that nations have been constructed out of ethnic materials is quite different from the assertion that nations have always existed. In my view, while the inalienable links between ethnies and nations need to be recognized, the assertion that nations have always existed is deeply problematical. There are some scholars who have taken this position. For example, Greenfield's (1992) work on the first expression of national sentiment in England in the early sixteenth century presents a wealth of literary evidence to support her argument. Others who have taken this position, that is, nations are much older than Gellner would like to believe, include Adrian Hastings (1997). He argued that one can find features of nation and national sentiment at least from the later medieval period. I would like to state that one problem with these formulations is that there is a kind of reading back into the formation of the 'old' nations the assumptions of modern nationalism. One finds operation of 'retrospective nationalism' in these formulations. As Reynolds argued, this perspective on nations prevents us from appreciating the ideas and sentiments of the early (or later) Middle Ages for what they were in themselves, without imposing a retrospective relationship between the medieval 'people' and their kingdom on the one hand and the modern 'nation' and its state on the other (1984,

p. 253). He also finds highly problematical the idea that nations are objective realities existing through history. As Reynolds noted, 'A more fundamental distortion arises from the fact that belief in the objective reality of nations inevitably diverts attention from itself: since the belief that nation exists is seen not as a political theory but as a mere recognition of fact' (1984, p. 251).

Furthermore, such a formulation makes an assertion that has not been conclusively established. When one argues that nations have been present for long, one needs to substantiate it. As Johnson (1995) argued, it tends to *assume what has to be proved* and its tendency to posit a historical continuity, given the silences and complexities of the historical evidence, is at best problematic. Apart from agreeing with the above formulation, I would also like to argue that conflating nations with ethnies as they existed before would do serious conceptual violence, though the nation, as stated earlier, needs to be built on certain existing cultural resources (such as traditions, myths, symbols etc.). There is a strong need to make a clear conceptual difference between the two. Although there are certain things common between them such as sense of shared history, identifying name, myths of common origins, traditions, customs and beliefs, there are certain clear distinguishing marks. For example, nation is characterized by certain features that an ethnie lack – a clearly delimited territory or 'homeland', a public culture, economic unity and legal rights and duties for everyone (Smith 1998, p. 196).

Coming to the issue of ethnic roots of nation, it needs to be dealt with the seriousness it deserves. Any modernist account of nations and nationalism would be poorer if it does not properly account for durability and widespread appeal of nation. This can be done, in my view, if it takes into consideration the importance of unifying memories and myths, symbols and values and traditions, stuff that make up an ethnie. A modern nation needs not only be a territory, economy, legal code and so on, it can also be an ethnic foundation that is able to mobilize and integrate diverse social and cultural elements. One can, for example, speak with some authority of a French or English ethnie that formed the core of French and English kingdoms by the fifteenth century. As Smith argued, national intellectuals play an important role in selecting and elaborating appropriate folk tales, ballads, epics, customs and rituals that are then weaved into a continuous dramatic narrative of the 'rediscovered' nation (1998, p. 13). This would mean making a selection between alternative traditions and events, ironing out inconsistencies and contradictions. The aim is to put together the different cultural elements in a dramatic narrative form that inspires and mobilizes the members of the ethnic to return to ancestral ways and ideas in order to create a modern nation. This is what many painters and poets, musicians and novelists in the late eighteenth-, nineteenth- and early twentieth-century Europe and America laboured to re-present in their tableaux of an imagined national past, on the basis of the historians' and philologists' researches (Einstein 1947, Rosenblum 1967). The essential point that needs to be underscored is that the significance of the past (recognizing the ethnic roots of modern nation) that embodies collective memories and a communal standard for inspiring and motivating the collectivity to aspire for a modern nation must be appreciated. Visions of a heroic past are constantly invoked to provide a solid and secure base for a modern nation. For example, the Davidic kingdom in ancient Israel became a source of inspiration in the early Haskalah (Enlightenment) movement in the early nineteenth-century German and Polish Jewry and the post-Vedic era of classical city (Eisenstein-Barzilay 1959, Meyer 1967). States on the Ganges similarly served to inspire a Hindu Indian national revival in the late nineteenth century (Sakai 1961). These visions of a past are placed in the context of a wider myth of origin and descent, which becomes the nationalist charter myth of the nation, instead of being isolated traditions or variants thereof, recorded in ancient epics, sagas and folktales (Smith 1988, p. 12). One has only to consider the strong attachment communities like the Afrikaners, Basques, Tamils or Sikhs have to their ethnic histories and cultures, to realize that over and above the other goals they may serve, nationalist regeneration, for example, they are end-values in themselves. As groups and groups of people define themselves in ethnic terms, the ethnic roots of the nation become increasingly visible, forcing even those groups that defined themselves in civic terms to regard themselves increasingly as ethnic nations, as happened in the late nineteenth-century France (Smith 1986). One point that needs to be taken note of at this juncture is that usually there would not be an agreement between different classes and groups within an ethnic group about the selection of cultural elements for nationalist regeneration. There would be frequent contestation about which elements need to be taken as the most authentic expression of their ethnic status. This does not, however, detract from that fact that the ethnic past serves as a model for inspiring a nationalist regeneration. As Smith reminded us, Western societies were historically formed around 'ethnic cores' – dominant ethnies that originated or founded the community and supplied most of the elite personal of the State, as was the case in the first national States – England, France, Holland, Spain and Sweden – as well as in Hungary and Poland (2001, p. 101). Furthermore, he argued that even an immigrant nation like the United States was created by the elites of a dominant Protestant British ethnic, although its ethnic character was subsequently transformed by waves of immigration on a large scale (p. 101). For him all nations and nationalism are, at root, 'ethnic' and any distinction between 'ethnic' and 'civil' nationalism is sociologically misleading.

Therefore, for Smith, the study of ethnies (the French term for ethnic community) becomes central to the understanding of why and how particular nations have emerged. He sees clusters of myths, symbols, memories, values and traditions emerging from the shared experiences of several generations of cohabiting populations, as the defining cultural elements from which ethnic groups emerged, and it was the revolutionary nature of the economic, administrative and cultural transformations that took place in the seventeenth- and eighteenth-century Europe that brought culture and ethnic identity to the fore as a basis for polity formation. This provided the context in which nations emerged drawing heavily on the cultural resources of ethnic communities. The sharing of traditions, myths, symbols, common sense of ancestry and so on became a central cultural resource to be put to effective use by nationalists in the formation of nations.

In this connection, the important point that Smith raises is that the elements that are sought to be re-appropriated and reconstructed from the ethnic past to bolster nationalist strivings must resonate with large numbers of the designated 'co-nationals', failing which any nationalist project is bound to fail. As he argued, 'If they are not perceived as authentic in the sense of having meaning and resonance with the "people" to whom they are addressed, they will fail to mobilize them for political action' (1998, p. 198).

This is where similar arguments advanced by some scholars on nationalism and nation also become quite significant. For example, Armstrong, who broadly subscribes to the ethno-symbolic approach, argues that the symbols, myths and communication that defined an ethnic identity in the pre-modern times are also the defining characteristics of the political community of nation. For Armstrong, symbols are quite significant in the sense that they act as 'borders' distinguishing the self from the others. Equally important are the legitimating myths. In his own words, 'The legitimating power of individual mythic structures tend to be enhanced by fusion with other myths in a *mythomoteur* defining identity in relation to a specific polity' (1982, p. 8). Myths have an immense power in the sense that they generate great passion among the members. As he would like to argue, the recital of myths can engender an intense awareness among group members of their 'common fate', by which is meant the extent to which an episode 'arouses intense affect by stressing individuals' solidarity against an alien force, that is, by enhancing the salience of boundary perceptions' (1982, p. 9). What is important to recognize in this formulation is that the elements of collective passion and attachment that are ignored in the Gellnerian account of the growth of nation (despite his laboured defence) are given adequate treatment. These elements play a crucial role in the growth of nationalist consciousness. It seeks to explore the reasons for 'continued emotional attachment of the people to their ethnic communities and nations and for their capacity for fanatical terrorism and self-sacrifice' (Smith 2001, p. 59). This, however, does not mean that 'objective' factors (political and economic factors) are ignored. An understanding of the working of subjective factors would help us enter the 'inner worlds' of ethnicity and nationalism (p. 57). Nationalist efforts are directed at making an effective use of these aspects of social and cultural existence. This provides an important corrective to the Gellnerian account of nationalism that primarily looks at nations in a deeply functionalist and instrumentalist posture underplaying the relevance of symbols, myths and communication that formed the core of an ethnic identity and from which nations began to take shape in the context of industrialization and modern world.

It is indeed true that more evidence needs to be gathered to identify the channels through which ethnies are transmitted and transformed into modern nations. However, ignoring the ethnic links of modern nation will not enable us to appreciate the passions that nationalist efforts arouse. Gellnerian account of nationalism can be made more meaningful if this glaring anomaly, that is, neglect of ethnic roots of nations, is rectified.

REFERENCES

Anderson, B. 1991. *Imagined Communities: Reflections on the Origin and Spread of Nationalism*. London: Verso.

———. 1992. Science, politics, enchantment. In J. A. Hall & J. C. Jarvie (eds), *Transition to Modernity: Essays on Power, Wealth and Belief* (pp. 202–232). Cambridge, UK: Cambridge University Press.

Armstrong, J. 1982. *Nations before Nationalism*. Chapel Hill, NC: University of North Carolina Press.

Barzilay, I. E. 1959. National and anti-national trends in the Berlin Haskalah. *Jewish Social Studies*, 21, 165–192.

Breuilly, J. 1993. *Nationalism and the State*. Manchester, UK: Manchester University Press.

Diaz-Andreu, M. & Smith A. D. 2001. Nationalism and archaeology. *Nations and Nationalism* (Special Issue), 7(4), 34–41.

Einstein, A. 1947. *Music in the Romantic Era*. London: J. M. Dent & Sons.

Elster, J. 1983. *Explaining Technical Change*. Cambridge, UK: Cambridge University Press.

Geertz, C. 1973. *The Interpretation of Culture*. London: Fontana.

Gellner, E. 1964. *Thought and Change*. London: Weidenfeld and Nicolson.

———. 1983. *Nations and Nationalism*. Oxford, UK: Basil Blackwell.

———. 1987. *Culture, Identity and Polities*. Cambridge, UK: Cambridge University Press.

———. 1994. *Encounters with Nationalism*. Oxford, UK: Basil Blackwell.

———. 1996. Reply to critics. In J. A. Hall & I. C. Jarvie (eds), *The Social Philosophy of Ernest Gellner* (pp. 625–687). Amsterdam, Netherlands: Rodopi.

Giddens, A. 1985. *The Nation-State and Violence*. Cambridge, MA: Polity.

Greenfield, L. 1992. *Nationalism: Five Roads to Modernity*. Cambridge, MA: Harvard University Press.

Hastings, A. 1997. *The Construction of Nationhood: Ethnicity, Religion and Nationalism*. Cambridge, UK: Cambridge University Press.

Hechter, M. 1975. *Internal Colonialism: The Celtic Fringe in British National Development, 1536–1967*. London: Routledge and Kegan Paul.

Hobsbawm, E. 1990. *Nations and Nationalism since 1780*. Cambridge, UK: Cambridge University Press.

Horsman, M. & Marshall, A. 1994. *After the Nation-State*. London: Harper Collins.

Johnson, L. 1995. Imagining communities: Medieval and modern. In S. Forde (ed.), *Concepts of National Identity in the Middle Age* (pp. 1–19). Leeds, UK: School of English, University of Leeds.

Kedourie, S. (ed.). 1998. *Elie Kedourie, 1926–92: History, Philosophy and Politics*. London: Frank Cass.

Kohl, P. & Fawcett, C. 1995. *Nationalism, Politics and the Practice of Archaeology*. Cambridge, UK: Cambridge University Press.

Kumar, D. V. 2006. *Modernisation and Ethnicity*. New Delhi: Mittal Publications.

———. 2008. Engaging with modernity: Need for a critical negotiation. *Sociological Bulletin*, 57(2), 240–254.

Mann, M. 1984. The autonomous power of the state: Its origins, mechanisms and results. *European Journal of Sociology*, 25(4), 69–78.

Meyer, M. A. 1967. *The Origin of the Modern Jew: Jewish Identity and European Culture in Germany, 1749–1824*. Detroit, MI: Wayne State University Press.

Mouzalis, N. 1998. Ernest Gellner's theory of nationalism: Some definitional and methodological issues. In J. A. Hall (ed.), *The State of the Nation: Ernest Gellner and the Theory of Nationalism* (pp. 158–165). Cambridge, UK: Cambridge University Press

Nairn, T. 1977. *The Break-up of Britain: Crisis and Neo-nationalism*. London: Verso.

O' Leary, B. 1998. Critical reply. In J. A. Hall (ed.), *The State of the Nation: Ernest Gellner and the Theory of Nationalism* (pp. 40–48). Cambridge, UK: Cambridge University Press.

Reynolds, S. 1984. *Kingdoms and Communities in Western Europe, 900–1300*. Oxford, UK: Clarendon.

Rosenblum, R. 1967. *Transformation in Late Eighteenth Century Art*. Princeton, NJ: Princeton University Press.

Sakai, R. (ed.). 1961. *Studies in Asia*. Lincoln, NE: University of Nebraska Press.

Shils, E. 1957. Primordial, personal, sacred and civil ties. *British Journal of Sociology*, 7(3), 13–45.

Smith, A. D. 1973. Nationalism, a trend report and annotated bibliography. *Current Sociology*, 21(3), 18–26.

———. 1983. *Theories of Nationalism*. London: Duckworth.

———. 1986. *The Ethnic Origin of Nation*. Oxford, UK: Oxford University Press.

———. 1988. The myth of the 'modern nation' and the myth of nation. *Ethnic and Racial Studies*, 11(1), 1–25.

———. 1998. *Nationalism and Modernism*. London: Routledge.

———. 2001. *Nationalism*. Cambridge, MA: Polity.

Van den Berghe, P. 1978. Race and ethnicity: A sociological perspective. *Ethnic and Racial Studies*, 14(4), 401–411.

———. 1979. *The Ethnic Phenomenon*. New York: Elsevier.

———. 1995. Does race matter? *Nation and Nationalism*, 24(2), 357–368.

6

Ethnicity, famine and the state

I

Natural calamities, including earthquakes, cyclones, hurricanes, typhoons, drought and famine, have been a regular and frequent phenomena human beings have always had to contend with. There is hardly any part of the world that can be said to be free from natural calamities. Earthquakes in Iran and Japan, cholera epidemic in Peru, drought in African countries, Hurricane Erick in Hawaii, and volcanic eruptions in Philippines and Alaska are only a few examples of natural disasters. India has had its own share of them. Typhoons in Orissa Coast (1999), earthquakes in Latur (1993) and Bhuj (2002), and floods in West Bengal and Assam have left a trail of destruction in the recent past. It has been observed that the frequency of calamities has actually increased in the past 50 years or so (Glickmen et al., 1994). The North-East of India, too, has been experiencing calamities of enormous magnitude. Floods have been a major occurrence in Assam. There have been recorded floods in

1240, 1570, 1642, 1786, 1781, 1825, 1842, 1862, 1867 and 1870 in Assam (Nag 2008, p. 19).

Along with floods, famines have been a regular feature of the history of North-East India. Manipur, Nagaland and Mizoram have frequently experienced famines. While some of the famines such as the one which took place in Mizoram called Mautam are regarded as natural, other famines are essentially a result of activities of unscrupulous elements. For example, in Manipur, food scarcity occurred during the early 1940s because of the fact that Marwari and Sikh merchants bought up all the rice produced in the valley and sent it outside during the Second World War for higher profits. This created a huge food shortage in the state and unleashed a strong reaction from the people, especially the womenfolk who organized an all-women movement against the export of local rice by outside traders (called *Mayangs* by the Meiteis, original inhabitants of Manipur).

While the North-East has not seen any dearth of natural calamities, what is glaring is that there has not been any systematic attempt *to relate these calamities to significant sociopolitical developments that followed those calamities*. This chapter seeks to do that. It looks at the sharpening of ethnic consciousness that generated a protracted ethnic movement following the occurrence of a famine called Mautam in the Mizo hills in 1959. The Mautam famine proved to be a catalyst in sharpening the ethnic consciousness, which was in a rudimentary stage among the Mizos. One of the first accounts of Mautam famine was J. D. Baveja's monograph (1970). However, this monograph came to be seen more as an ethnographic narrative on the history and society of the Mizos rather than on the famine itself. Nevertheless, this monograph 'immortalised the association of the Mizo people with bamboo flowering' (Nag 2008, p. 22). There have been a few notable attempts at presenting a comprehensive picture about the famine (Nag, to mention one). However, as mentioned above, they did not look at how the famine in the Mizo hills had tremendous sociopolitical consequences in terms of, for instance, consolidation of ethnicity among the Mizos, which generated a protracted ethnic movement for greater political autonomy for the Mizos.

Before we embark upon the main task of understanding the famine and relating it to the socioeconomic and political developments that took place in Mizoram, a word about the Mautam famine is definitely in order here. The Mautam famine takes place at regular intervals and is considered a hugely amazing phenomenon. It results from the flowering of bamboo plants and consequent multiplication of rats. The rats relish the bamboo fruit which contains the seed. They come out over ground even at the risk of being killed by serpents and other animals to relish the bamboo fruit. This significantly enhances the reproductive health of the rodents. As a result, they become prolific breeders, increasing their population substantially. After exhausting the bamboo fruit, they have nowhere to go but on to the paddy fields and eat away the produce meant for human beings, thereby creating a situation of severe food shortage. Knowledge about this famine was originally transmitted through oral tradition. The tribal leaders would share their knowledge of this with others. Despite the fact that it happened at periodic intervals in Mizoram, not much understanding of this peculiar phenomenon and its consequences is available. The flowering of bamboo is a peculiar phenomenon in the sense that the entire forest of bamboo plants flowers at the same time, which is why such an event is called 'gregarious flowering'. They die at the same time too. Records of bamboo flowering stretch back as far as ninth century A.D. when a particular variety of bamboo called phyllostachys bambusoides flowered in Japan (International Network for Bamboo and Rattan). Scientifically the bamboo flowering phenomenon is called 'synchronic masting' (Vishwanathan 1997, pp. 204–208). This term referred to the synchronized production of seeds at long intervals by a population of plants, and masting was considered the accurate term. However, the term *flowering* was used by colonial authorities which gained wide acceptance.

The gregarious flowering of bamboo increases the supply of rodents, which is described as a carnival for the animals (Vishwanathan 1997, p. 207). Referring to the relationship between bamboo flowering and multiplication of rats, Ghose says that the fruit has high protein, nearly 12 per cent, and very high starch content of about 50 per cent besides Vitamin A which helps augment the fertility of rodents (*The Telegraph* 2001).

The story of the journey of the Mizo hills from a mere district in the state of Assam to a separate state is all about how ethnicity was effectively used a mobilizing tool by the Mizos (Kumar 2009). Although there were many crucial points in this journey, the most prominent one was the Mautam famine in 1959 and its aftermath. The situation that followed the occurrence of the famine in 1959 provided the context in which ethnicity or ethnic consciousness was effectively used for the achievement of their socioeconomic and political demands. The significance of understanding this situation also lies in the fact that it would provide a huge empirical support to the oppositional approach to ethnicity that seeks to synthesize the primordial and instrumental approaches to ethnicity and thereby provides an effective explanatory framework for a proper and meaningful understanding of ethnicity.

Before we understand what the oppositional approach is all about and how it can help us appreciate the intensification of ethnic consciousness in the wake of Mautam famine in 1959 in Mizoram, a word or two about Mizoram and the Mizos is required. Mizoram (formerly known as Lushei Hills) is located in the North-Eastern part of India. It is surrounded by Tripura and Bangladesh in the west, Manipur and Assam in the north and Burma in the east and south. It has enjoyed and continues to enjoy strategic importance as it shares its international borders with Bangladesh and Burma.

The term *Mizo* has two parts: Mi and Zo. Mi means 'man' and zo means 'highland'. Therefore, Mizo literally means people living in highland (Verghese and Thanzawna 1997, p. 45). There are different theories that explain the origin of Mizos. One of the most widely accepted theories is that Mizos were said to have originated from 'Chhinlung' in South-West China (Nunthara 1996, p. 39). From there they were said to have migrated to Burma where they lived for a long time. Acute poverty caused by the famine called 'thingpui tam' forced them to move towards the present-day Mizoram (Vanlawma 1972). In terms of their racial roots, they are said to be the Assamese-Burman subgroup that had branched off from the Tibeto-Burman group of the main Tibeto-Chinese race. Some authors have classified them as Tibeto-Burman because of the affinity of the language, even though they have described them as people who once lived in Chhinlung (as stated above). However, it needs to be stated quite clearly that in view of the absence of the records or documentary proof regarding any contacts between this group and the people of other countries or states or areas, it is extremely difficult to trace the exact history of the Mizos.

Mizo is a generic term that refers to various groups such as Lushai, Lakhers, Pawi, Chakma and Hmars who claim to possess distinct cultural traditions and identity from each other. Lushais (the most dominant among Mizos) constitute about 68.89 per cent, and they inhabit the major portion of the heartland of Mizoram. Pawis, Lakhers, Chakmas and Hmars constitute about 6.9, 5.1, 7.14 and 2.65 per cent, respectively, and mainly made the periphery either in the north or the south of Mizoram as their homeland (Singh 1994, p. 12).

II

At this juncture, it would be pertinent to have a preliminary idea of what ethnic group and ethnicity mean to us. The following definitions of ethnic group would serve the purpose, though there are quite a few equally or more appropriate definitions of ethnic group (Barth 1969, Glazer and Moynihan 1975)

Paul Brass defines an ethnic group as 'any group of people dissimilar from other people in terms of objective cultural criteria and containing within its membership, either in principle or practice, the elements of complete division of labour and for reproduction forms an ethnic category' (Brass 1991, p. 19). As far as ethnicity is concerned, De Vos defines it as 'subjective, symbolic or emblematic use by a group of people . . . of any aspect of culture, in order to differentiate themselves from other groups' (George De Vos 1975, p. 16). Paul Brass, however, modifies the last phrase to read 'in order to create internal cohesion and differentiate themselves from other groups' (Brass 1991, p. 19). We keep the above definitions in view as we proceed along.

The oppositional approach advocated by Edward Spicer (1971) seeks to synthesize two powerful approaches, primordial and circumstantial, in explaining the ethnic phenomenon. These two approaches have so far been powerful approaches (Glazer and Moynihan 1975). However, in my view both these approaches have some serious limitations and, therefore, the need for the oppositional approach.

The primordial approach tries to account for strong ethnic attachments on the basis of their ineffable affective, that is, their deep emotional importance for members. This affective significance most generally surrounds images of the group's distinctive past, thus indicating that there is a historical dimension of primordialism (Connor 1978, Greeley 1974, Issacs 1975, Smith 1981)

The circumstantial approach, on the other hand, perceives ethnic group solidarity as resulting from the context. Scholars using this approach contend that certain circumstances lead to the strategic selection of ethnic identity as a means of attaining desired political, economic and other social goals (Bell 1975, Cohen 1974, Hector 1974, Young 1976).

In my understanding neither approach alone would satisfactorily explain the salience of ethnic solidarity. The primordial approach, while it can explain the persistence of ethnic identity over time, fails to account for the fluctuation in the intensity of ethnic solidarity. This is because it does not take into account the relevance of social, economic and political circumstances for enhancing or reducing ethnic solidarity. The circumstantial approach, while it can explain why ethnicity fluctuates in intensity as it adequately takes account of changing circumstances, tends to ignore the affective significance of ethnic ties and, hence, cannot explain persistence, sometimes over centuries, of ethnic solidarity.

Therefore, a model that can systematically combine these two into a unified explanatory framework would be of immense use in understanding the persistence and growing salience of ethnicity. Such a model can be derived from the 'oppositional approach' originated by Edward Spicer (Spicer 1971, pp. 795–800).

Although the oppositional approach was not originally intended to integrate the above two approaches – primordial and circumstantial – it nevertheless provided the basis for such an integration (Kumar 2006, 2009).

According to the oppositional approach, ethnic groups are viewed as persistent identity systems. Examples such as Jews, Irish, Welsh and various tribal groups in the North-East come to mind. They have persisted over long periods of time despite adverse circumstances. These groups have deep ineffable affective importance for their members. What, however, sustains and accentuates such an importance is the oppositional process. The sociocultural, economic and political opposition experienced by a group from the other, usually dominant groups, is mainly responsible for this. Various symbols such as language are frequently used to assert their distinct identity. This approach can successfully explain not only the persistence of an identity but also the fluctuation in the intensity of attachment to that identity. The degree of an ethnic group's solidarity will vary in direct proportion to the amount of opposition it encounters; the greater the opposition, the greater the degree of solidarity and, conversely, the lesser the amount of opposition, the lesser the degree of solidarity.

What role does primordialism play in this model? It acts as an intervening variable. The greater the degree of opposition, the greater the primordial sentiments endangered and the greater the degree of ethnic solidarity experienced by the group. Opposition, then, does not lead directly to ethnic solidarity but operates indirectly through the psychological mechanism of primordial sentiments. When opposed, members of an ethnic group will conjure up images of their glorious past, often intertwined with images of their ancestor's deprivation and suffering that helps further to strengthen ethnic ties. Thus, in this model primordiality is causally tied to the circumstantial variable of opposition.

We now arrive at the following hypothesis: the greater the opposition – social, political, economic or some combination thereof – perceived by an ethnic group, the greater the degree to which its historical sense of distinctiveness will be aroused and, hence, the greater its solidarity or the more intense its movement towards redress (Spicer 1971).

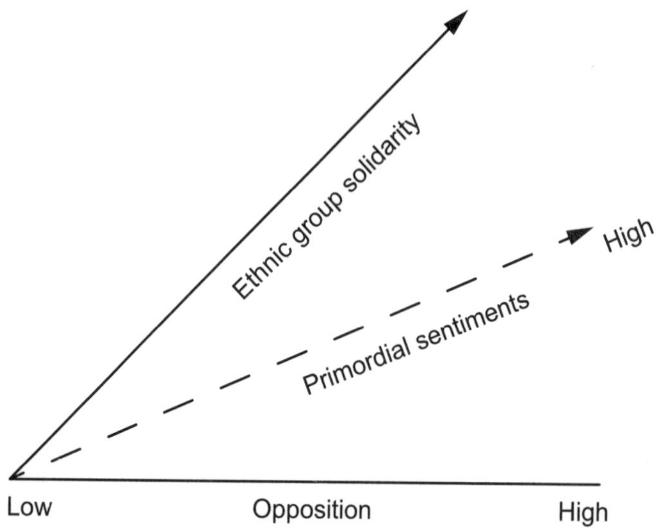

Let us keep the above hypothesis in view while examining the heightened ethnicity in the wake of famine and its aftermath in Mizoram. The famine and the subsequent frustrating experiences that the Mizos were forced to suffer provided the oppositional context wherein the historical sense of distinctiveness was aroused and efforts began to be made for the redressal of their grievances by using ethnicity as an effective mobilizing tool. What we are looking at is how a natural calamity, by providing the right context, solidified ethnicity, generating a protracted ethnic movement.

This chapter could be viewed as partly historical and partly socio-anthropological as it seeks to make use of historical material in its theoretical appreciation of the phenomenon of ethnicity.

III

In this section we try and acquire some appreciation of historical background of the Mautam famine as this would enable us to get a proper perspective on the phenomenon of the famine in Mizoram and its distinctive and destructive nature.

Before that, a word or two about the very meaning of famine is required. *International Encyclopaedia of Social Sciences* defines a famine as shortage of food so extreme and protracted as to result in widespread persisting hunger, notable emaciation in many of the affected population and a considerable elevation of the community death rate attributable to starvation. Famines, it needs to be noted, are not new to societies. What is distinctive about the modern-day famines is that it now affects only the poor and marginalized sections of the society, whereas in the past it affected the whole society. Famines could be the result of both natural and artificial causes. Natural causes would include drought, floods, earthquakes and so on, whereas artificial ones would include wars, conquests and so on. Walford listed twelve causes classifying them into natural causes beyond human control and artificial causes within human control (1878–1879, pp. 433–526).

Famines have always been a central fact of human existence. The major famines in history were the Irish famine of 1845–1852; in Greece and Holland during the Second World War; Persia, Egypt, in 1897; Brazil, in 1877; and Morocco, in 1977–1988.

Two kinds of famine

Coming to Mizoram, two kinds of famine have been identified, which are associated with two kinds of bamboo species, *thing* and *mau* in Mizoram. The one associated with the former is called *thingtam* and the latter is *mautam*. Thingtam would occur after every thirty years and mautam after every fifty years. In terms of impact, thingtam is localized and, hence, not quite destructive, whereas the latter leaves its impact over a much larger area and therefore highly feared. Mautam attracts a larger number of rats and lasts longer while thingtam is of shorter duration. It was found out that the thingtam famine did not affect the Lakher tribes of hills because the *thing* variety of bamboo was not found in those areas (Rokhuma 1988).

It is interesting to note that with the help of Mizo elders, the British administrators drew up a calendar of famines and also the flowering periodicity from 3 to 120 years (see Table 6.1 and 6.2, respectively; Nag 2008).

Table 6.1

Nature of famine	Year
Mautam	1860–1861
Thingtam	1880–1881
Mautam	1910–1911
Thingtam	1930–1931
Mautam	1960–1961
Thingtam	1977–1978
Mautam	2007–2008

Table 6.2

Species	Period between flowerings indicated in number of years
Bambusa balcooa	35–45
B. bamboo	45–48
B. blumena	45–100
B. polymorpha	35–60
B. textilis	Regularly found to flower; does not die after flowering
B. tulda	30–60
B. vulgaris	Rarely found to flower
Cephalostachyum pergracile	Sporadic
Dendrocalamus asper	Not known
D. giganteus	40–65
D. latiflorus	Sporadic
D. strictus	40-65
Gigantochloa	50–60
G. Levis	Sporadic, not fatal
G. pseudoorundinacea	50–60
Guadua angustifolia	Not Known
Melocanna baccifera	35–36, 48, 60
Ochlandra travancorica	7–23
Phyllostachys pubescens	67 and sporadic
P. bambusoides	60 (and 120)
Thyrsostachys siamensis	35-50

At this stage it would be interesting to look at the *change* in the nature of encounter between the Mizos and the colonial administration as a result of the famine in 1881 and its aftermath. It was not in the original scheme of things of the colonial administrators that they would invade and occupy the hills. They realized that nothing substantial could be procured by spending time, energy and money on trying to occupy the hill areas as 'the hills were not a land of flowing milk and honey, no glittering outcrops to raise, no telling indications of reservoirs of endless oil' (McCall 1949, p. 65). What virtually forced them to enter the hills was the frequent raids by the Mizos in search of human head, materials and other necessary things to the villages located in the foothills. People living in the foothills were constantly in fear of being attacked any time by the tribals. The British administration saw no other option but to send forces to conquer and subjugate them. The declared policy was to civilize the uncivilized and to bring some semblance of normalcy in the neighbouring villages. In pursuance of this policy they sent repeated expeditions to conquer and subjugate the tribals. However, to their chagrin they found out that the Mizos were made of sterner stuff and it was not easy to subjugate them. Nevertheless, the British did not give up and continued their expeditions. In a sudden turn of events in the 1880s the British found out that a large number of Mizos were coming down in search of food and other necessary things. At first it was thought by the people that it was a raid by the Mizos as usual. Later it was realized that these Mizos were very desperate and they were coming down for their survival. Enquires made by the British officers revealed that it was the result of famine that broke in the Mizo hills in 1881. The famine of 1881 debilitated the Mizos significantly. The economy was shattered. Thousands of people died and many others were afflicted with a number of diseases. The famine was followed by plague and other such epidemics. A number of people migrated to the other parts of the North-East, especially Manipur. They were in a state of destitution. The famine resulted in severe food shortage, and even the chiefs were selling all their belongings to purchase necessary items for their survival. This became a huge dilemma for the British. It was about whether to extend necessary help to them who were in desperate need or let them suffer. There were those who argued that no help should be extended to them because once they were enabled to survive the famine they would go back to their old practice of conducting raids on the villages and plundering things from them. There were others who took a different position, which was that the more viable option of winning over the tribals on a long-term basis was to extend timely help when they desperately required. Famine was the best time to do so as everything they had was lost in the famine. This position was well supported by the Lieutenant-Governor of Bengal, Sir Bailey. He argued that the best way of developing friendship with the Mizos was to come to their rescue during the occurrence of a very important event such as a famine (Chatterjee 1999, pp. 152–153). He took the initiative in arranging for the necessary storage of food grains. In this process he took care that the chiefs were not given much importance as he wanted to ensure that the benefactors should realize who were extending help actually.

The policy of coming to the aid of the Mizos earned their goodwill towards the British. The Mizos were very convinced by the positive attitude of the British towards them as reflected in their readiness to help them when they needed it the most. The kind of relief provided by the British was unprecedented in their history. A Deputy Commissioner who felt elated at the response of the Mizos wrote, 'A feeling of confidence and gratitude prevailed among the western Clans: the fear and distrust of Europeans diminished to such an extent that the Assistant Commissioner of Hailakandi was invited in some cases to visit the punjis. This is noteworthy, for the Lushais are very jealous in excluding Europeans, and are very superstitious in believing that cholera always follows in their wakes' (cited in Nag 2008, p. 133). This resulted in the changing image of the British administration in the eyes of the Mizos. They began to see the colonial administrators in a more positive light and as benevolent. This change in image actually helped the British in consolidating their hold over the Mizo tribals.

The missionaries had difficulty in introducing Christianity in the Mizo hills in the beginning. They would be ridiculed, abused and even chased away. However, because of the role they played when the famine took place in 1881, they gradually gained the support of the Mizos. Missionaries showed readiness in helping the needy people in terms of supplying food materials, giving medicines to those affected by cholera and other diseases, and extending moral support to them.

Since the kind of famine that occurred in Mizoram was strange to the British, they began to make efforts to understand this. The first report about the bamboo flowering was prepared by Captain McCuloch from Manipur. It was, however, not well-received. Commenting on the report, F. C. Hennieker, the Superintendent of Lushai Hill said, 'I gather that Colonel McCuloch had not actually seen the phenomenon of which he writes. He was describing it from native accounts' (cited in Nag 2008, p. 66), thereby implying that his report lacked scientific grounding. It was felt that the understanding arrived at by Colonel McCuloch regarding the famine was not quite correct, may be because he depended too much on interlocutors who were not sufficiently well-versed in English. Otherwise he would not have attributed the famine to the swelling of the bamboo species, as he had done in his report. He also did not understand the connection between bamboo flowering and multiplication of rats. Subsequently Government of Assam prepared the Annual General Administration Report that dealt with the issue of famine in the Mizo hills. However, this report too did not reflect a correct picture of the famine as it did not appreciate the phenomenon of bamboo flowering and rat–famine connection. One had to wait till the arrival of two missionaries, J. H. Lorraine and E. W. Savidge, on 11 January 1894, for a proper understanding of the famine. They missed the famine of 1861 and 1881 but were witness to the bamboo flowering that took place in 1911–1912. After witnessing the famine, Lorraine wrote: 'Exactly the same thing happened before and after the seeding of the mau bamboos in 1911 and it is because I lived through the heartbreaking experiences of the mautam famine of 1911–1912 that I am so desirous that the government should do something to provide against the thingtam famine which according to universal Laushai belief is fast approaching' (cited in Nag 2008, p. 69).

The Mizo history was full of struggles. However, their struggle against famine constitutes perhaps the most important of all of them. The famine has had such a huge impact on their lives that one could hear the Mizo elders talking about 'before or after that great famine'. Everything revolved around the famine. If a young boy or girl lived through a famine, they were quite sure that the boy or girl would was a lucky person and he or she would live to see another famine.

The famine that occurred as a result of bamboo flowering is a huge environmental event having serious socioeconomic and political consequences. Apart from the fact that it created enormous food shortage as a result of which people died of hunger, it had other repercussions. Bamboo constitutes an essential part of lives of Mizos. Traditionally their houses are made of bamboo. Their kitchen utensils, hunting bows and arrows, spinning gadgets for textiles, pots for carrying water baskets, beds and smoking pipes, all are made of bamboo. They were badly hit when bamboos began to rot and die. During the time of flowering, before they could make use of bamboo, rats would eat away the flowers and the plants would die. Mizos would be forced to migrate to the hills of Manipur and Assam plains and to other places following the famine in search of food. The socio-psychological experience of being uprooted from their traditional habitat was too horrifying to bear. The reduced population of Mizos made themselves vulnerable to subjugation and enslavement by the neighbouring tribes. People would die of starvation. Diseases would engulf people, leading to loss of precious human lives.

Another tragic consequence of the famine was the destruction of communitarian spirit for which the Mizos were traditionally known for. The service motive is embodied in the philosophy of Tlawmngaihna, which is the Mizo code of moral and good form. One cannot, for example, be regarded as Tlawmngai unless they are courteous, considerate, helpful, unselfish, courageous, industrious and ready to help others even at considerable inconvenience to themselves, and a man who practices the precepts of Tlawmngaihna is highly respected. This spirit began to weaken rapidly in the context of hardships that Mizos had to face. Since they were too preoccupied with their own survival, there was hardly any willingness or time to serve others. The loss of the communitarian spirit was one of the biggest losses that the elders always lamented. A number of fables, myths and stories are associated with the famine. The following stories convey the poignancy associated with the occurrence of a famine and serve as illustrations.

One of the stories was that there a was little girl brought up by her stepmother. During a famine the entire family of the girl moved from place to place in search of food. When other consumables were exhausted they entered the jungle and dug deep into the earth for hakai (a root resembling *yam*). However, a day came when even the jungle *yam* had been exhausted. All the family was left with was just one last dinner after which the entire family would have died of starvation. While the mother was cooking the last supper the little girl was getting desperate for food. She kept pestering her mother to hurry up and serve her the food. Enraged by the impatience of the girl, the stepmother hit the hand of the girl with the serving spoon severing her fingers from the hand. Hurt and tearful, the starving girl immediately turned into a bird and flew away. Since then she would fly from village to village and say *Ka hut, Ka hut* (Cuckoo, Cuckoo), which in Mizo meant, my hand, my hand (Nag 2008, p. 91).

The other story was about two orphan brothers, Thanghou and Liandou, who were moving from place to place in search of food in the immediate aftermath of a famine that occurred. They could not find any. At last, they saw a group of farmers carrying harvest and they felt elated. They rushed to that place. By the time they reached that place, they found that nobody was there. However, they continued their search as they thought at least some amount of grain would be left behind. At last, they found only a single grain of millet and since they were very hungry, both of them wanted to eat it. However, soon the brotherly love triumphed over starvation and they decided to share that single millet and save their lives for another day (Nag 2008, p. 91).

The Mizos soon realized that if they had to survive the famine the one thing they must do is kill the rats because it was the rats who were primarily responsible for eating their crops and creating food shortage. In December 1924, 45,000 to 50,000 rats were killed in Aizawl sub-division alone. This was the story of all the famines that had been recorded so far. Taking cue from the people, the colonial administration subsequently had officially launched a campaign for mass destruction of rats from 1925 onwards. During the rat famine of 1911–1912 that affected the Burmese side of the Mizo population also, the Government of Burma organized a great battle against the rodents and destroyed thousands of them (*Annual Report of the Baptist Mission Society*, South Lushai Hills, Assam, 1912).

IV

The Mautam famine that took place in 1959 in Mizoram proved to be a highly destructive event and also deeply consequential. It was destructive because it inflicted enormous damage in terms of loss of human lives and property, which was much higher than that of previous famines of 1881 and 1912, and it was deeply consequential because it led to the consolidation and strengthening of ethnic/nationalist consciousness among the Mizos in the aftermath of the famine. We will see how it happened.

By the time the famine occurred in 1959, neither the 'paternalistic' British nor the powerful chiefs were there (chieftainship was abolished in 1954). Even the missionaries who played a vital role in the previous famine in terms of providing relief left India. The Mizos were practically alone this time. They were heavily dependent on the Government of Assam (the Mizo hills were a district in the State of Assam) and looked to it for help and succour.

Around 1954 *rawte* (one variety of bamboo) started flowering leading to an enormous increase in rat population. By 1956 another kind of bamboo, locally known as *phulrua*, too started flowering, which intensified the crisis. That was the time when the Mizos expected the Assam government to readily come forward and help them. To their chagrin they found that the Assam government was not interested in taking any pre-emptive steps. On the contrary, to rub insult to injury, the minister concerned in the government of

Assam dismissed the whole idea of rats causing a famine as a tribal superstition (Nag 2008, p. 245).

The Mizo Union, which was the ruling party in the district council, began to take steps to pre-empt the hardship that the impending famine was likely to cause to its people. It passed the following resolution on 29 October 1958 and handed it over to the government of Assam. The resolution read as follows: 'With the flowering of bamboos in the Mizo district rat population has enormously increased and it is feared that in the next year (1959) the whole district would be affected. As a precautionary measure against the imminence of famine, following the flowering of bamboos, the District Council feels that the Government be moved to sanction to the Mizo District Council a sum of Rs 15 lakhs to be expended on a test relief measure for the whole of the Mizo district including the Pawi–Lakher region' (cited in Nag 2008, p. 248).

To the utter shock of the Mizos, this resolution was completely ignored by the Assam government, and no concrete steps were taken to deal with this impending crisis. In the meantime, the famine occurred in a phased manner. In 1958, famine was felt in areas lying to the east of Turint River. By 1959 it had affected the rest of the Mizo hills as well.

When the famine finally struck in 1959, the Assam government was caught completely unawares. Despite the fact that it received a series of requests from the Mizos through the District Council, it did not take any adequate precautionary steps. When it actually happened, it became alert and began to send relief measures. But the food and other materials could not reach the Mizo hills because of extremely bad road connectivity. The delayed reaching of relief supplies to the Mizo hills angered the Mizos to no end, forcing one of the members of the District Council to articulate their anger in the following manner: 'If we continue to be neglected, the people's feeling will be for secession from Assam' (Chaube 1973, p. 179). The considerable anger of the Mizos alerted the Assam government to some extent and sanctioned relief under various heads such as gratuitous relief, general relief, subsidy and so on. The bulk of the relief funds were spent by way of subsidy, on transport of grain, purchase of vehicles and petrol and construction of godowns for storage of rice.

The Assam government, however, did not want to send the relief through the District Council as it was in the control of Mizo Union that did not curry favour with the Assam government because of its secessionist orientation. Instead it involved a non-governmental organization called the Mizo National Famine Front (MNFF), which was formed with ostensible purpose of providing relief to the needy. This was headed by the charismatic Laldenga who was shrewd and extremely articulate. Along with the provision of relief to the distressed people, this organization had its own agenda of promoting anti-India feelings among the people by emphasizing the point that the Mizos could not expect to get satisfactory relief from the indifferent and callous Indian State and the Government of Assam.

In the meantime the Mizo National Famine Front (MNFF), which was started with the objective of helping the people during the famine, began to nurture political ambitions. With the support it gained as a result of its active involvement in the relief activities, it realized that it could transform itself into a political party. The indifference and apathy shown by the Assam government and the Indian State were politicized and interpreted as inflicting a direct insult on the dignity and self-respect of the Mizos as a distinct ethnic group. The Mizo National Famine Front transformed itself into the Mizo National Front (MNF), a political party, with the situation proving conducive for such a transformation. The MNF became increasingly aggressive in their denunciation of the neglect shown by both Indian and Assam governments on their plight. It stepped up its activity of indoctrination and mobilization of ethnicity to demand sovereignty. The distinct Mizo ethnicity was constantly harped on. MNF argued that the Mizos were a 'distinct nation created, moulded and nurtured by God and nature', and 'it considered the merger of Mizoram with the Indian Union as an expression of political immaturity, ignorance and absence of farsightedness' (Memorandum to the Prime Minister by MNF on 30 October 1965) and said that freedom was their basic human right. The memorandum submitted to the PM on 30 October 1965 sought to emphasize the distinctive character of Mizos as a separate nation. It said, 'The Mizos from time immemorial lived in compete independence without interference. Chiefs of the different clans ruled over separate hills and valleys with supreme authority and their administration was very much like Greek city states of the past. Their territory and every part thereof had never been conquered or subjected by the neighbouring state . . . the Mizo people are inseparably knitted together by their strong bond of tradition, custom, culture, language, social life and religion wherever they are (to emphasize *the separate ethnic character of Mizos*, italics mine). The Mizos stood as a separate nation even before the advent of British government, having a nationality distinctive and separate from that of India. In a nutshell they are a distinct nation, created, moulded and nurtured by God and nature. It is clear that in the aftermath of the famine and frustrating experiences of the Mizos, the kind of language that was used in the memorandum commanded huge popularity and legitimacy. A clear attempt was made to harp on the ethnic identity of the Mizos. Such an attempt became hugely successful in the context of enhanced ethnic consciousness.

The famine in 1959 provided the context in which articulation of Mizos as an ethnic group were in danger gained considerable legitimacy. The logic of ethnicity was made an effective instrument of mobilization. The separatist identity was harped on, and their separateness was shown as the real cause of relative deprivation. Inadequate relief provided during the famine was a clear manifestation of the fact that they were as an ethnic group subjected to deprivation. It shows how a peripheral region inhabited by a distinct ethnic group was thrown to the mercy of a natural disaster without any help from the government. This could happen only because the Mizos were the 'Other' vis-à-vis the rest of India in physical type, language and culture. The MNF mobilized people by feeding them on their deprivation and neglect on the part of the Indian government.

The MNF became successful in its attempt to appropriate the nationalist discourse and in the process marginalized other political formations such as the Mizo Union. It had already warned the people against merging with India. It warned that the big nation would turn oppressive. The neglect shown by the Indian State only confirmed their suspicion. The MNF used all features of nationalist discourse on an impoverished group of people whose plight was worsened further by the famine. For an exhausted population the nationalist discourse articulated by the MNF seemed quite legitimate and plausible. What the dominant class of chieftains could not achieve in the 1940s was realized in the 1960s using the same rhetoric. As Nag put it succinctly, 'A natural disaster made all the difference' (Nag 2008, p. 272).

Adding fuel to the fire was another critical event – the passing of the Assamese Language Bill on 24 October 1960. It made Assamese the official language of the state. Mizos began to fear that their traditional and cultural life would be destroyed if they were forced to learn the Assamese language. Language holds extremely affective significance for the users. Any attempt to deny the right to learn their language would always be restricted. This is what happened in the case of Mizoram too. When Assamese was made the official language, the disillusionment the Mizos felt following the Mautam famine became more acute. As said previously, it was like adding fuel to the fire. With such a move on the part of the Assam government, Mizos were convinced that unless they fought for their autonomy and acquired it their distinctiveness as Mizos would be gradually eroded and lost forever.

To be able to effectively control the underground and the violent activities of the MNF, the Central Government embarked upon the regrouping of villages in Mizoram. The regrouping of villages meant the whole population of some villages were lifted and physically relocated at one place. The regrouping of villages was yet another critical event in the post-independent history of Mizos, which accentuated the sense of opposition among Mizos towards the 'Other' (the Indian government). Although the declared objectives of the regrouping of villages were to provide protection to the villages, facilitate economic development and improve communication facilities, the real objective of that step was to exercise greater control over the activities of the underground elements of the MNF. What happened in the process was that considerable amount of hardship was inflicted on the now-regrouped Mizos. The shifting of villagers was compulsory and people suffered physically and psychologically. People were forced to leave their native villages where they lived for years. The scars of such forceful eviction are still evident in the psyche of Mizos. Many of them suffered from severe destitution, from which they never really recovered.

The important point to be remembered is that some of the events, the Mautam famine in 1959 being the most important of all, which took place in Mizoram actually accentuated the sense of opposition among Mizos towards the Indian State, Assam government and 'outsiders'. This led to intensification of ethnic sentiments that in turn gradually led to one of the most ethnic-based autonomy movements in Mizoram. The distinctiveness of Mizos was constantly stressed. In fact, Mr. Laldenga was reported to have commented sometime in 1982 that the 'crux of the problem was the different racial origin of the Mizos and their struggle to maintain their distinct identity' (Chakraborty 1994, p. 119). Ethnic group as a primordial group holds ineffable and affective significance for its members. However, for ethnic sentiments to get activated and ethnic solidarity to be intensified there have to be predisposing circumstances such as perception of opposition by members of any ethnic group vis-à-vis other groups as had happened in the case of Mizoram. This explains a heightened sense of ethnic consciousness that grew markedly during the 1960s and 1970s, manifesting itself as a call for rebellion to achieve secession. Lack of political autonomy and abominable economic situation made Mizos' sense of opposition very acute, intensifying their ethnic sentiments and solidarity.

To sum up, it would be clear from the foregoing discussion that the famine of 1959 provided the oppositional context in which the distinctive ethnic identity of the Mizos was stressed and acted as a trigger for the Mizos to launch a protracted ethnic agitation against an oppressive and indifferent Indian state. The abominable conditions that developed in the aftermath of the famine and the reluctance of the State to come to the rescue of the people resulted in deep hurt and pain. There was a deep-rooted realizationthat only because of their ethnic distinctiveness they were ignored by the Indian government. The oppositional approach that we made use of in understanding the sharpening of ethnic consciousness offers us a better explanatory framework as it combines context and sentiments (which is how it should be) as we have seen in the context of Mizoram.

REFERENCES

Annual Report of the Baptist Mission Society, South Lushai Hills, Assam. 1912.

Barth, F. 1969. Introduction. In F. Barth (ed.), *Ethnic Groups and Boundaries* (pp. 9–38). Boston, MA: Brown.

Baveja, J. D. 1970. *Mizoram: The Land Where Bamboo Flowers*. Guwahati, Assam, India: Assam Publication Board.

Bell, D. 1975. Ethnicity and social change. In N. Glazer & D. P. Moynihan (eds), *Ethnicity: Theory and Experience* (pp. 141–174). Cambridge, MA: Harvard University Press.

Brass, P. 1991. *Ethnicity and Nationalism: Theory and Comparison*. New Delhi: Sage.

Chakraborty, P. 1994. Autonomy movements: A case study of the Mizos. In R. N. Prasad (ed.), *Autonomy Movements in Mizoram* (pp. 109–122). New Delhi: Vikas Publishing.

Chatterjee, S. 1999. *A History of the Mizo Economy* (Vol. 1). Jaipur: Printwell.

Chaube, S. K. 1973. *Hill Politics in North-East India*. Delhi: Orient Longman.

Cohen, A. 1974. Introduction. In A. Cohen (ed.), *Urban Ethnicity* (pp. 9–35). London: Tavistock.

Conner, W. 1978. A nation is a nation, is a state, is an ethnic group, is a.... *Ethnic and Racial Studies*, 1(4), 377–400.

de Vos, G. 1975. Ethnic pluralism. In G. de Vos & L. Romanucci-Rovi (eds), *Ethnic Identity: Cultural Continuities and Change* (pp. 12–24). Palo Alto, CA: Mayfield.

Glazer, N. & Moynihan, D. P. 1975. Introduction. In N. Glazer & D. P. Moynihan (eds), *Ethnicity: Theory and Experience* (pp. 1–26). Cambridge, MA: Harvard University Press.

Glickmen, T. S., Golding, D., & Silverman, E. D. 1994. *Acts of God and Acts of Man: Recent Trends in Natural Disasters and Major Industrial Accidents* (Discussion Paper, CRM 1992–2000). Washington, DC: Centre for Risk Management.

Greeley, A. M. 1974. *Ethnicity in the United States: A Preliminary Reconnaissance*. New York: Wiley.

Hector, M. 1974. The political economy of ethnic change. *American Journal of Sociology*, 79(5), 1151–1178.

Issacs, H. R. 1975. Basic group identity: The idols of the tribe. In N. Glazer & D. P. Moynihan (eds), *Ethnicity: Theory and Experience* (pp. 45–72). Cambridge, MA: Harvard University Press.

Kumar, D. V. 2006. *Modernisation and Ethnicity*. New Delhi: Mittal Publications.

———. 2009. Explaining Mizo ethnicity: The relevance of oppositional approach. *Man in India*, 89(1–2), 37-50.

McCall, A. G. 1949. *Lushai Chrysalis*. London: Luzac.

Nag, S. 2008. *Pied Pipers in North-East India: Bamboo-Flowers, Rat-Famine and the Politics of Philanthropy* (1881–2007). New Delhi: Manohar.

Nunthara, C. 1996. *Mizoram: Society and Polity*. New Delhi: Indus Publishing.

Rokhuma, C. 1988. *Tam Do Pawlin Engnge An Tih?* (What Is Anti-Famine Organization Doing?). Aizawl, Mizoram: Author.

Singh, S. N. 1994. Hmar autonomy movement. In R. N. Prasad (ed.), *Autonomy Movements in Mizoram* (pp. 123–132). New Delhi: Vikas Publishing.

Smith, A. D. 1981. *The Ethnic Revival in the Modern World*. Cambridge, UK: Cambridge University Press.

Spicer, E. 1971. Persistent identity systems. *Science*, 4011(67), 795–800.

Vanlawma, R. 1972. *My Country and I*. Aizawl, Mizoram: Zoram Printing Press.

Verghese, C. G. & Thanzawna, R. L. 1997. *A History of the Mizos* (Vol. 1). New Delhi: Vikas Publishing.

Vishwanathan, S. 1997. *A Carnival of Science*. Delhi: Oxford University Press.

Walford, C. 1878–1879. Famine of the world: Past and present. *Journal of Royal Statistical Society*, 41, 433–526.

Young, C. 1976. *The Politics of Cultural Pluralism*. Madison, WI: University of Wisconsin Press.

7

Modernization and ethnicity

The context of Telugus in Bengaluru

The problem

The central problem I would like to explore in this work is whether modernization has led to the disappearance of ethnic consciousness or not. I do this in the context of Telugus in Bengaluru by examining whether people who demonstrate attributes of modern consciousness also demonstrate attributes of ethnic consciousness. In other words, I would like to examine whether those who think along modern lines (to be clarified shortly) also think along ethnic lines, that is, respond to sociocultural, economic and political issues from an ethnic (Telugu) point of view. If they do, it would mean that modernization has not led to the disappearance of ethnic consciousness.

The context

The essential motivation arises from the resurgence of ethnicity in the 'modern' and contemporary world. Ethnicity which is supposed to have faded into oblivion has shown an implacable tendency to persist and in fact assume greater predominance. Both Marxists and non-Marxists (to follow the conventional categorization) have argued that ethnicity would decline in its significance in the conditions of modernization. Marxists would contend that the inevitable development of class consciousness, which is taken as an expression of modernity, would strike at the very root of ethnicity. Non-Marxists would argue that the development of rationality and scientific outlook, as reflected in the privileging of reason over faith and belief in the modern world, would lead to the considerable emasculation of 'traditional' social bonds, of which ethnic attachments are a prime example.

However, one can notice spectacular manifestations of ethnicity in the contemporary world. One can rationalize them in terms of inadequate modernization in the case of traditional societies. How would one justify them in case of even the 'modern' and advanced societies? This is what motivates me to engage myself in a re-problematization and re-examination of the relationship between modernization and ethnicity. I do so in the context of Telugus in Bengaluru. Before I do so, it is imperative that we look at the concepts modernization and ethnicity, which are supposed to be theoretically loose and methodologically unwieldy.

The incisive sociological analyses of modernity and modernization emanated from the works of Marx (1859), Durkheim (1964) and Max Weber (1922). The Communist Manifesto is usually regarded as the first major sociopolitical affirmation of modernity. The frequent appearance of terms such as 'modern industry', 'modern worker', 'modern State power' in the writings of Marx are in a sense a celebration of modernity. Capitalism, despite all its negative features, is regarded as a highly modernizing tool. In the writings of Durkheim, the movement of societies from the stage of mechanical solidarity to that of organic solidarity engendered by the development of division of labour is essentially a process of modernization. The enunciation of the processes of secularization and rationalization in the writings of Max Weber indicates that the process of modernization is on. More recently, Habermas (1987) and Giddens (1990) have enriched our understanding of modernity. To the credit of these celebrated thinkers, it must be stated that they are also incorrigible critics of modernity. Marx speaks of 'alienation', Durkheim of 'anomie' and Weber of 'disenchantment of the world'. The Frankfurt school theorists have made a scathing critique of modernity and of its tendency to homogenize and destroy differences.

Coming to the empirical processes of modernization, different conceptualizations have made their appearance. Daniel Lerner (1958), Black (1966), Levy (1966), Talcott Parsons (1971), Hoselitz (1960), Smelser (1969), Bendix (1964), to mention only a few, have defined modernization in ways they thought appropriate. In this work I have taken Alex Inkeles's (1966) notion of modernity to understand the relationship between modernization and ethnicity. The attributes that a modern person is supposed to possess, as described by him, are enumerated below.

The notion of ethnicity been understood differently by different scholars; Barth (1969), Bromley (1974), Cohen (1974), Glazer and Moynihan (1976), Smith (1981), Brass (1991), to mention only a few. The tendency to conflate ethnicity with race and nation is objected to on the ground that each of them has its own history and trajectory and any conflation and subsumption of one under the other would ignore the specificities associated with each of them.

As for literature that deals with the relationship between modernization and ethnicity, it has been found appropriate to divide it broadly in terms of two theories: theories of decline and theories of persistence. The former is further divided into Marxist expectancy and liberal expectancy. Similarly the latter is further subdivided into primordialism and instrumentalism.

Coming to the theories of decline, the basic argument put forward is that ethnicity would decline in its significance. Reasons for decline could vary depending on which expectancy one subscribes to. Marxists, for example, would argue that ethnic, religious, racial and national attachments will decline with the growth of capitalism (a modern socioeconomic). Classes would assume central importance. According to liberal expectancy, ethnicity would decline because of significant changes in political, social, cultural and economic spheres.

As for theories of persistence, their proponents argue that ethnicity would persist. Only its form and articulation may undergo changes. Again reasons could vary depending on whether one takes a primordialist position or an instrumentalist position. Primordialists would argue that ethnicity would persist because an ethnic group holds ineffable and affective significance for its members. It is a given, requiring description rather than explanation. It is bound to persist even in the context of modernization. Among primordialists, one can include Shils (1961), Barth (1969), Geertz (1975), Bromley (1974), Issacs (1975) and so on. The instrumentalist position holds that ethnicity is an artefact, created by individuals or groups to bring together a group of people for some common purpose. It is used as an instrument to mobilize members of a group to achieve socioeconomic and political objectives. Therefore, ethnicity would always persist as circumstances needing ethnicity continue. Among scholars associated with this position one can include Cohen (1974), Hector (1975), Bell (1975), Glazer and Moynihan (1963), Rex (1970), Smith (1981), Roosens (1989), Brass (1974) and so on. Variants of this approach, such as rational-choice theory and resource–competition theory, are also examined. The oppositional approach, which is supposed to provide the basis for the synthesis of primordial and instrumental approaches, is also dealt with.

As stated earlier, I would like to examine the relationship between modernization and ethnicity in the context of Telugus in Bengaluru. It would be pertinent to know whether those who exhibit attributes of modern consciousness also exhibit attributes of ethnic consciousness. In other words, I would like to examine whether those who think along modern lines (to be clarified shortly) also think along ethnic lines, that is, respond to sociocultural, economic and political issues from an ethnic (Telugu) point of view. If they do, it would mean that modernization has not led to the disappearance of ethnic consciousness.

One clarification needs to be made here. Our engagement with Telugus in Bengaluru should not lead to the conclusion that ethnic conflicts exist in Bengaluru or that there is a strong ethnic assertiveness among Telugus and therefore we are proceeding to study them. Absence of strong ethnic assertions and/or ethnic conflicts does not mean the absence of ethnic consciousness. The latter can exist even in the absence of the former.

In order to enquire into this problem, I would like to find out:

1. Whether political preferences of modern persons are determined by their ethnic background.
2. Whether those who think along modern lines want to see the Telugu community become stronger politically thereby reflecting deep ethnic consciousness.
3. Whether they support any movement to mobilize Telugus politically.
4. Whether they want Telugu associations to promote political awareness among Telugus.
5. Whether they (modern persons) want to depend on Telugu associations for economic assistance.
6. What medium of instruction they want their children to study in.
7. Whether Telugu associations support the idea of Telugu schools and are satisfied with the number of Telugu schools available in Bengaluru.
8. Whether their sociocultural choices such as marriage are determined by one's ethnic background (Telugu).
9. Whether they see the need for greater interaction among Telugus.
10. Whether they feel closer to Telugus than they did before they migrated to Bengaluru.

Mode of enquiry

The main mode of enquiry used in this work is the questionnaire method, given the paucity of time and resources at our disposal.

I have also used every possible opportunity to attend Telugu association meetings, functions, small get-togethers to gather a variety of insights.

The questionnaire was originally distributed to 160 respondents belonging to different gender, educational and occupational groups. My main task is to find out, as stated at the outset itself, whether people who think along modern lines also think along ethnic lines or not. Therefore, my first task is to find out people who exhibit modern attitudes. The questionnaire contains five questions, the responses to which help us do that. To construct the questionnaire, I have taken a cue from Alex Inkeles (1966), who has done path-breaking work on the modernization of man in six developing countries. Some attributes that can be regarded as characteristic of a modern person may include faith in science, orientation towards the present rather than the past and so on.

Each question carries three responses and the responses were rated on a scale of 1 to 3. The 'modern' response carries 3 points, the 'neutral' response carries 2 points, and the 'non-modern' response carries 1 point. The points secured by a respondent from all the questions are added and then divided by the number of questions (5), which gives the mean score obtained by each respondent. Anybody scoring above 2 is regarded as 'modern'. These questions deal with readiness for new experience and change, orientation towards the present rather than the past, significance of planning and so on.

After identifying the respondents who demonstrate attributes of modern consciousness I will examine their views on social, cultural, economic and political issues concerning Telugus, which would indicate the presence of ethnic consciousness or the lack of it. To do this, I designed twelve questions, responses to which would indicate if respondents continue to be conscious of their ethnic identity. If they do so, then it is clear that modernization has not contributed to the disappearance of ethnic consciousness. Ethnic identities continue to exist even in the context of modernity.

Each of these questions carries again three responses. The response that indicates the presence of ethnicity carries 3 points, neutral response carries 2 points, and the response that indicates their negation of ethnic consciousness carries 1 point. Then the points secured by a respondent are divided by the number of questions (10), which gives the mean score of the respondent. Anybody scoring above 2 would be regarded as a person who is deeply conscious of his or her identity as a Telugu. He or she would be regarded as a person who demonstrates attributes of ethnic consciousness along with the attributes of modern consciousness.

Modernization: empirical context

Our primary task is to find out the relationship between modernization and ethnic consciousness. Whether modernization leads to disappearance of ethnic consciousness or not is a task that we have set for ourselves. If people who exhibit modern qualities also demonstrate a strong sense of ethnic awareness, then it would mean that modernization has not led to the disappearance of ethnic awareness.

However, what qualities should a person possess if he or she is to be regarded as a modern person. This is a question that does not lend itself to an easy answer. As mentioned above, we have made use of Alex Inkeles's understanding of modernity of man. We have already dealt with it at length in the methodological discussion and also with the fact that his conceptualization of modernity need not be unproblematical. However, his understanding of modernity can be taken as a good starting point. We would, therefore, use his conceptualization of modernity in our empirical work.

Here, we briefly deal with the sources of modernization that Alex Inkeles refers to. He mentions the following sources: education urbanization; mass communication; the development of national, state and its associated apparatuses of government bureaucracy; political parties and campaigns; military and para-military units and the like (Inkeles 1966, pp. 151–163).

Given proper quality, education's impact on modernization is bound to be greater. Education fosters national and scientific outlook. However, little or no change towards modernity is evident in the more traditional schools that devote themselves mainly to passing on religious practices or to inculcating and preserving traditional folklore and skills. This is a characteristic of schools not only at the primary level but also of those offering nominally advanced education.

Urban environment is considered an important source of modernization. It provides the context that exposes men to a variety of situations, ideas and opinions. Men are relatively freed from obligations imposed by institutions such as family, kinship and so on. However, it must be noted that this may not necessarily always occur. Sociological studies conducted reveal the fact that cities are also characterized by the prevalence of traditional institutions.

Then comes the role of mass communication in spreading modernizing influences. Alex Inkeles contends that almost all studies of the growth in individual modernization show that those who are more exposed to the media of mass communications have more modern attitudes (Inkeles 1966, pp. 151–163).

Government bureaucracy, political parties' campaigns, military and paramilitary and the like are extremely important in spreading modern attitudes. They have become powerful channels through which modern attitudes are transmitted to people at large.

It hardly needs to be emphasized that the modern factory and administrative enterprise play a significant role too. Certain features of the modern factory are relatively invariant, and they communicate the same message, no matter what the cultural setting in which they may be installed. In addition, a factory guided by modern management and personnel policies will set its workers as an example of national behaviour, emotional balance, open communication and respect for the opinions, the feelings and the dignity of the workers, which can be a powerful example of the principle and practice of modern lives.

Although there are a number of qualities associated with modernity we have taken the help of only a few qualities, as already mentioned in the Introductory chapter, to enable us distinguish a modern person from a traditional one. Although the questionnaire was originally distributed to around 200 persons, we have been able to get duly completed responses from only about 160. As stated earlier, we are essentially concerned only with those who exhibit modern qualities. Our first task is, therefore, to find out those who exhibit such qualities and then we will try to find out whether they exhibit any attitude that reflects their ethnic consciousness. If they do so, it is indicative of the fact that modernization does not lead to disappearance of ethnic consciousness.

To identify those who exhibit modern qualities, we have followed the 3-point scale, as stated above. Each question carries three responses, which are given 3, 2, 1 points. The 'modern' response carries 3 points, the 'neutral' response carries 2 points and the 'non-modern response' carries 1 point. The points secured by a respondent from all the questions are added and then divided by the number of questions (5 questions), which gives the mean score obtained by each respondent. Anybody scoring above 2 would be regarded as modern and only his or her responses to the questions that deal with ethnicity are taken into account.

We now proceed to find out the modernity of a person through some of the issues mentioned above.

Readiness for new experience and change

The willingness to face new experiences and expected/unexpected changes is one of the attributes of a modern person, as stated in the beginning of this chapter. In our day-to-day discourse also, we would regard any person who would not like to move from one place to another as conservative and backward-looking. Anybody who is keen on changing places and exposing himself to different experiences is usually regarded as dynamic and, therefore, modern-looking. Therefore, we have structured the question in this way

Table 7.1 Readiness for new experience and change

Given a chance, would you like to change the occupation and move to another place even if It means getting exposed to a new experience altogether?	Number	Percentage
(A) Yes, ready for a change	90	56.25
(B) It is difficult to answer	28	17.50
(C) No, it would be difficult to adjust to new situations	42	26.25
Total	160	100

As we have already mentioned, the modern response (A) carries 3 points, the neutral response (B) carries 2 points and non-modern response (C) carries one point. This pattern of quantification has been applied to data presented in all the tables in this chapter.

As Table 7.1 indicates 90 (56.25 per cent) out of 160 respondents have indicated that they are keen to be exposed to a new experience and change, whereas 42 (26.25 per cent) respondents have said that they are not willing to experiment with anything new. The rest of them are undecided about this.

Diversity of opinion on issues

The second attribute that we have considered to be characteristic of modern person is that he or she would recognize the diversity of attitude and opinion around him, rather than closing himself off in the belief that everyone thinks alike and indeed just like him. Any person claiming to be a modern would generally allow for the possibility of diversity of opinion on issues. The ability to see different alternatives is an illustration of one's openness, which is taken as an essential attribute of modernity.

Table 7.2 Diversity of opinion on issues

Would you allow for the possibility of diversity of opinion on issues?	Number	Percentage
(A) Yes, there is always the possibility of having a difference of opinion on issues	110	68.75
(B) It is difficult to answer	30	18.75
(C) No. There is no possibility for any diversity on some issues, for example, reservation policy	20	12.50
Total	**160**	**100**

As many as 110 out of 160 (68.75 per cent) respondents believe that there is always the possibility of having a diversity of opinion on issues such as reservation policy whereas 20 (12.50 per cent) respondents believe otherwise. We have chosen the reservation policy as an example because it is a controversial issue and one should be open-minded enough to understand various points of view. About 30 respondents have found it difficult to answer this question.

Issues that are of interest

A person could also be regarded as modern if he or she reflects on lager issues and holds opinions on them instead of confining him or herself to his or her immediate environment. A modern person would like to concern him or herself with the larger environment. The tendency to restrict oneself to the 'local' environment is regarded as an expression of one's inward-looking nature, which does not coexist happily with the culture of modernity. We have therefore asked the following question:

Table 7.3 Issues that are of interest

Which of the following issues interest you most?	Number	Percentage
(A) Those concerning the state and the country	56	35.00
(B) It is difficult to answer	12	7.50
(C) Those concerning the neighbourhood and town	52	32.50
Total	**160**	**100**

A total of 56 out of 160 respondents said that issues concerning the state and the country interest them most whereas 52 respondents said that they are concerned with the neighbourhood and the town. This does not seem to be too surprising because most of us would like to know what is happening in our immediate neighbourhood.

Orientation towards the present

Orientation towards the present rather than towards the past would also indicate whether a person is modern or not. Therefore, they are asked whether they ponder over the mistakes they made in the past so much so that they neglect things that are presently happening.

Table 7.4 Orientation towards the present

Would you ponder over the mistakes you made in the past so much so that you neglect things that are presently happening?	Number	Percentage
(A) Does not happen, I always look ahead	75	46.87
(B) It is difficult to answer	32	20
(C) To a great extent yes. It happens quite often	53	33.12
Total	**160**	**100**

A person who has imbibed the qualities of modernity would always like to look ahead and deliberate upon things that are likely to happen in the future instead of squandering away time thinking about something that happened in the past over which he or she has no control. According to this, 75 out of 160 would come under our understanding of modernity. However, those who brood over the past at the cost of doing something worthwhile in the present or future also constitute a significant number (53 or 33.12 per cent). Those who have refused to say anything categorical constitute 25.65 per cent of respondents. Such a large number of respondents have found it difficult to answer possibly because it involves experiences too personal to be shared with anybody else.

Faith in the ability to control environment

A modern man is also expected to have faith in his ability and efficiency to control environment. The question designed to address this aspect is as follows.

Table 7.5 Faith in the ability to control environment

Do you believe that someday people will fully understand the reasons behind, and control, natural phenomena such as floods etc.?	Number	Percentage
(A) Yes. I think some day people will do that	90	56.25
(B) It is difficult to answer	12	7.50
(C) No. It is impossible	58	36.40
Total	**160**	**100**

One of the negative effects of modernization is the unbridled desire of people to control and devastate environment to satisfy material interests. However, as the above table indicates, 90 out of 160 believe that someday people will definitely understand and control natural phenomenon, whereas 58 stated clearly that it is impossible to control natural phenomena. However, this finding has to be taken with a pinch of salt as even the most modern person would not like to believe that humans can control natural phenomena such floods. What is surprising, in fact, is that 90 out of 160 respondents believe that it is possible to control natural phenomena. This certainly represents incorrigible optimism.

Then we have proceeded to the first empirical step of identifying the persons who demonstrate attributes of modern consciousness. A total of 120 respondents have emerged as modern as they have secured a mean score more than 2. As stated previously, we are keen on knowing only their views about different sociocultural, economic and political issues that reflect their ethnic consciousness. The general finding that emerges from this is that 90 respondents have secured a mean score more than 2. It clearly indicates that majority of our respondents, though being modern, have retained their ethnic consciousness.

We wanted to find out the total number of people who would fall under the 'modern' category. For this we have taken into account all those who have secured a mean score of more than 2. Our findings reveal that 120 respondents have secured a mean score more than 2 (total score secured by each respondent and divided by the number of questions), which means their attitude can be described as 'modern'. We now proceed to find out whether these 120 respondents are conscious of their Telugu identity (ethnic consciousness) as revealed through their responses to sociocultural, economic and political issues. In other words, we would like to know whether these respondents, despite being modern, think along the ethnic lines. If they do so, it can be taken to mean that modernization has no impact on their ethnic consciousness. Our findings and interpretations in this regard are as follows:

To find out whether these 120 respondents keep ethnicity as the basis when they express their views on sociocultural, economic and political issues, they have been asked twelve questions. Each question carries three responses: respondents' desire to exercise their choice on the basis of their ethnicity (Telugu), a neutral response and they are opposed to it. They carry 3, 2, 1 points, respectively.

The reason these questions were chosen is that the responses to these questions would clearly indicate whether a person is conscious of his or her ethnic background. For example, the question whether somebody would vote for a Telugu candidate in an election is clearly designed to find out whether his or her political references are determined by the ethnic background. Similarly, the response to the question whether one supports the idea of Telugu schools would clearly tell us whether they view such schools as an affirmation of their Telugu identity. It they in favour of such schools, it is a clear support to one of the important symbols of Telugu identity.

Ethnicity and the political context

One key factor responsible for the growing ethnic assertiveness is a desire on the part of a group to acquire political power. Political power is the ultimate power that every group desires to possess. Without political power it is extremely difficult to satisfy socioeconomic needs. Possession of political power places a group in an advantageous socioeconomic situation. In a democratic setup, the route to political power is election. Whether elections are really the yardstick to test the health of democracy is a question that need not detain us here as political scientists are in a better position to answer that question. It is indubitable that unlike in totalitarian systems where political power is acquired more through force than any democratic means, in a democracy one needs to become part of the electoral politics to be able to entertain hopes of acquiring political power. Keeping this in view, we asked our respondents the following question.

Table 7.6 Voting behaviour and ethnicity, Part 1

If a Telugu candidate is pitted against a candidate from the other linguistic communities, who would you vote for?	**Number**	**Percentage**
(A) I would vote for the Telugu candidate because he would take care of our interests	86	71.67
(B) It is difficult to answer	12	10.00
(C) I would vote for a candidate whose ideology and programmes I like	22	18.33
Total	**120**	**100**

The response indicating ethnic consciousness (A) carries 3 points, neutral response (B) carries 2 points and response negating ethnicity (C) carries 1 point. The same pattern of quantification has been applied to data presented in all the tables.

A huge majority of respondents (86 out of 120) responded that they will vote for a Telugu candidate if he is contesting in an election. Only 22 out of 120 respondents said that they would vote on the basis of ideology and programmes.

We also wanted to know what they would do if there were no Telugu candidate. Our finding in this case is mentioned as follows.

Table 7.7 Opinion regarding Telugu candidate

What would you do if no Telugu candidate is contesting?	Number	Percentage
(A) Would vote for a different person who enjoys support among Telugus	64	53.33
(B) It is difficult to answer	21	17.50
(C) Does not matter, I would look for an alternative	35	29.16
Total	**120**	**100**

As many as 64 respondents indicated they would like to go for a person who enjoys support among Telugus. This is apparently based on the belief that a person acceptable to Telugus would not have any discriminating attitude towards Telugus. About 35 respondents said they would look for an alternative. However, this has to be taken with a pinch of salt as they perhaps would not like to be accused of being politically irresponsible. As many as 21 respondents said the question was difficult to answer. It is interesting that more people found it difficult to answer this question than the previous one possibly because they are unable to decide clearly on the possibility that there may not be Telugu candidate contesting the elections. If a Telugu candidate is not contesting, the question of voting a candidate would be determined by one's perception of how broad-minded that candidate happens to be. Then we wanted to know whether they wished to see the Telugu community become politically stronger.

Table 7.8 Preference to see the Telugu community politically stronger

Would you like to see the Telugu community stronger politically than it is now?	Number	Percentage
(A) Yes. The Telugu community should get stronger and stronger	93	77.5
(B) It is difficult to answer	7	5.83
(C) I am satisfied with the political status of the community	20	16.66
Total	**120**	**100**

The fact that a huge number of respondents, 93, would like to see the Telugu community become stronger is a reflection of their proclivity towards their ethnic identity. Only 20 respondents have said that they are satisfied with the existing status of their community. Acknowledgement of satisfaction with their current status could as well be a reflection of indifference to their status. What this researcher noticed was that people were not willing to express their views freely because they had to interact with members of other communities in different situations and they did not want to be exposed. It took considerable effort on the part of the researcher to make respondents answer this question. However, once sufficient confidence was instilled by the researcher, they came out freely. An overwhelming number of respondents said they would also support any movement to mobilize Telugus politically.

Table 7.9 Mobilization of Telugus along political lines

Do you support any movement to mobilize Telugus politically?	Number	Percentage
(A) Yes. I do support any such movement	75	62.50
(B) It is difficult to answer	15	12.50
(C) No. I do not see any reason for that	30	25
Total	**120**	**100**

As many as 75 (62.50 per cent) respondents said they would support any movement that mobilizes Telugus politically. The number is quite significant in view of the popular conception that Bengaluru is supposed to offer a congenial atmosphere for individual growth and an expression of support for political mobilization seems irrelevant. Still when people are asked a direct question like this, they are willing to come out openly in favour of supporting such movements. This only underscores strong ethnic attachments.

In one of the social gatherings, this researcher intentionally broached this topic. Although they were taken a little aback by this question, they slowly began to discuss this with a great deal of passion. One teacher who was present there said that this was a good question and they should think seriously about it. When people are mobilized along the lines of caste, language, region everywhere, why should Telugus lag behind? However, this was immediately objected to by another who said that there was simply no reason to support any mobilization of Telugus for political reasons.

Majority of our respondents would like the Telugu associations to promote political awareness among them.

Table 7.10 Promotion of political awareness by Telugu associations

Do you think Telugu Associations should try to promote political awareness among Telugus?	Number	Percentage
(A) Yes. They are well-equipped	86	71.66
(B) It is difficult to answer	14	11.68
(C) No. They should confine themselves to cultural activities	20	16.66
Total	120	100

The fact that 86 (71.66 per cent) respondents have expressed a preference to see that identity-based associations such as Telugu associations play a role in the promotion of political awareness among Telugus, which is reflective of their deeply entrenched ethnic feelings. They do not seem to recognize the fact that the main objective of such associations is to promote cultural activities. However, 20 respondents did take cognisance of this.

Majority of our respondents also said they would like to depend upon Telugu associations for economic betterment.

Table 7.11 Extension of economic assistance by Telugu associations

Do you think Telugu associations should come forward to extend economic assistance to the needy Telugus?	**Number**	**Percentage**
(A) Yes, definitely. They should do whatever is possible to help Telugus economically	102	85.00
(B) It is difficult to answer	8	6.66
(C) No. They should confine themselves to cultural activities	10	8.34
Total	**120**	**100**

An overwhelming number of respondents (102, 85 per cent) have said that Telugu associations should come forward to extend whatever assistance they can to the needy Telugus. About 10 respondents said that they should confine themselves to cultural activities. This may be taken as an expression of one's ethnic consciousness. However modern a person may be, the tendency to make use of the identity-based associations is unmistakable from the above. Some of the respondents who have some knowledge of the situation in countries like USA, Britain and so on have told me that the use of one's ethnic networks happens in those countries also and, therefore, it should not surprise anybody if there is an expression of expectations that these networks should come to the aid of Telugu people in needs. The fact that such a feeling is expressed by a modern-inclined person is sociologically significant.

Ethnicity and the sociocultural context: the issue of language

The attachment to one's own language is a reflection of one's ethnic consciousness. In fact, language constitutes the most important ethnic symbol. We therefore proceed to elicit their views on the issue of language. It goes without saying that attachment to one's own language is usually quite strong. No amount of modernization would weaken it. The desire to use one's mother-tongue (or native language) for communication or to express themselves even when they are required to speak in other languages, as it happens in the case of migrants such Telugus in Bengaluru, would reflect on the sense of belonging one has to their language. This is why we would like to know what they think and do about a situation where they are required to speak the local language which is not their mother-tongue.

As a starting point on this issue, we have asked the following question.

Table 7.12 Preference for the medium of instruction

Which medium of instruction would you like your children to study?	Number	Percentage
(A) Telugu medium	34	28.34
(B) It is difficult to answer	12	10.00
(C) English medium	74	61.66
Total	**120**	**100**

When it comes to the question of choosing the medium of instruction for their children, pragmatic considerations demand that it be English medium. English offers innumerable advantages and possibilities especially in the context of increasing globalization. It is common perception that anybody not studying in English medium would not only become the object of ridicule socially but deprive him or herself of the opportunity to climb to higher rungs at the socioeconomic ladder. This explains why a significant number of respondents (74) choose to send their children to English-medium schools. One can choose to speak in Telugu at home because it is a question of continuing allegiance to one's own most powerful symbol of identity. However, one feels compelled to refrain from it from those spaces (schools, offices etc.) where it could prove relatively harmful. Therefore, ethnicity or expression of it tends to be highly contextualized.

The medium of instruction at schools happens to be one of the issues calling for attention from policymakers, administrators and academicians. Whether it should be English or one's own mother-tongue is the question that has not been satisfactorily answered. There are strong advocates for education in English as well as for education in mother-tongue. Proponents of English generally structure their arguments in terms of fact that it facilitates smooth interaction at both national and international levels, enables one to gain access to the latest scientific and technical knowhow and so on. On the other hand, the arguments put forward by the proponents of the mother-tongue as the medium of instruction are political. They believe advocacy of the mother-tongue would enable them to reap political benefits as the language is a deeply emotive issue. And if the objective conditions are favourable, it can be made more emotive than it normally is. In the context of real or perceived deprivation, mobilization of people along linguistic lines has proved to be very effective.

It would also be a matter of interest to know whether they support the idea of Telugu schools as a matter of expression of their ethnic sentiments.

Table 7.13 Support for Telugu schools

Whether you support the idea of Telugu schools?	Number	Percentage
(A) Yes. I strongly support that	85	70.83
(B) It is difficult to answer	12	10.00
(C) No. I am against that	23	19.16
Total	**120**	**100**

It is significant to note that though majority of them would otherwise like to send their children to English-medium schools as a matter of pragmatic considerations (in reply to the previous questions), they in principle support the idea of Telugu schools. As many as 85 (70.83 per cent) of respondents have supported the idea of Telugu schools. About 23 have expressed themselves strongly against that. The argument put forward by one of the respondents was that this would lead to ghettoization and the community would fail to develop a larger perceptive. This would also deny their children the opportunity of coming up the socioeconomic ladder. However, the fact that majority of them support the idea of Telugu schools may be attributed to their desire to see that the Telugu language gets the importance it deserves. One of the respondents who supported the idea of having separate Telugu schools said that despite the fact that the Telugu population constitutes a huge segment in the population of Bengaluru, it is unfortunate that sufficient number of Telugu schools do not exist. This deprives them of any opportunity to learn their mother-tongue. They fear that if this state of affairs continues, that is, absence of sufficient number of Telugu schools, unity among Telugus would progressively decline.

Although they harp on the Telugu language as a symbol of their identity, in common discourse, they in fact prefer to send their children to English-medium schools, as we have shown in Table 7.12. Expression of support for Telugu schools may be taken as an assertion of ethnicity as a politically meaningful proposition. However, sending their children to English schools may be taken as an expression of their pragmatism. Political leaders express such a context quite clearly. As one can notice in the case of Tamil Nadu,

West Bengal, UP and other states, they agitate for the introduction of local language as the medium of instruction and removal of English from schools, thus making a serious political statement and at the same time sending their children to the best missionary schools (where English is invariably the medium of instruction).

The researcher also noticed that in one of the association meetings, one speaker passionately argued for the starting of more Telugu schools in Bengaluru. Bengaluru being a huge city cannot cater to the needs of so many Telugus living there. This discourages a number of people from sending their children to Telugu schools as they are located far from their houses. However, it was later found out that his own children were studying in English-medium schools though one Telugu school was close to his house.

Continuing the discussion along similar lines, it will be interesting to know whether they are satisfied with the number of Telugu schools in Bengaluru. As mentioned elsewhere the number of Telugu schools in Bengaluru is around five (65 respondents say so), which includes primary and high schools.

Table 7.14 Satisfaction with the number of the Telugu schools

Are you satisfied with the number of Telugu schools?	Number	Percentage
(A) No. there should be more such schools	76	63.33
(B) It is difficult to answer	14	11.66
(C) Yes. It is more than enough	30	25
Total	**120**	**100**

The fact that more people would like to have more Telugu schools should not be surprising in the context of our explanation above. The plea for having more Telugu schools may not be in consonance with the context of modernity we are talking about. One can demand more Telugu schools without necessarily thinking that they would send their children to them. In one of the school meetings, where this researcher was present, the headmaster (who was one of our respondents) was happily conveying information to the students that there would be more

Telugu schools soon in Bengaluru, thanks to some committed Telugus who were trying to mobilize funds for the purpose. He spoke at length how important it was to have as many Telugu schools as possible to transmit Telugu language and culture. Schools are one of the important channels through which this can be done. He was imploring the student to become strong in the Telugu language as it is one of the most powerful symbols of one's identity.

We wanted to continue to elicit their views on why they attach importance, if at all they do, to Telugu. The following table deals with this.

Ethnicity and the sociocultural context: the issue of marriage

When it comes to the question of some of the personnel issues such as marriage, one's inclination towards one's group become most apparent. Although caste endogamy has weakened a little, it has not completely disappeared. Even among highly educated groups, one still notices that endogamy is practiced. This is because of the persistence of caste consciousness. It will also be quite useful whether the same would hold true in the case of an ethnic group such as the Telugu community. The following table shows data pertinent to this question. As far as marriage is concerned, most of the respondents said they would like to marry from the Telugu community itself. Illustrative evidence is provided as follows.

Table 7.15 Marriage choice

Would you like to marry/or marry off your children to somebody from a different linguistic group?	Number	Percentage
(A) No. That may cause many problems	87	72.50
(B) It is difficult to answer	13	10.83
(C) Yes. I do not mind if I get suitable choice	20	16.66
Total	**120**	**100**

As the above table clearly indicates 87 respondents (72.50 per cent) would not like to marry a person from outside the Telugu community because it may cause problems. Only 20 respondents do not seem to have any problem marrying a person from any other linguistic community.

In one of the cultural functions where this researcher happened to be present, there was discussion on this matter. One teacher who was working in a school expressed his dismay over the fact that there were growing intercommunity marriages (between Telugus and Kannadigas) and if this continued a day would come when it would become difficult to get an alliance for a girl or a boy. When probed further, he was opposed to it because apart from the reason mentioned above, it would also create some adjustment problems. It was also considered necessary to probe them on the need for greater interaction among the Telugus. The following table shows data pertinent to this issue.

Table 7.16 Need for a greater interaction among Telugus

Do you think there should be a greater interaction among Telugus?	Number	Percentage
(A) Yes. There is a strong need for that	102	85.00
(B) It is difficult to answer	5	4.17
C) No. It is not necessary	13	10.83
Total	**120**	**100**

Majority of our respondents feel there is a strong need for greater interaction among Telugus in order perhaps to consolidate themselves into a strong ethnic group. They believe that only by doing so would it be possible for them to gain political clout and economic resources. This was stressed at some of the association meetings, also where this researcher happened to be present. More interaction at social, cultural and political levels would lead to better understanding. The absence of any interaction, as some of them put it, would make them highly vulnerable to the ill-designs of the majority-language group. For the sake of strengthening cohesion among them, it is important they have more interaction within their community.

One of the school teachers told me that he did not know that there were Telugu associations and schools in Bengaluru till a few months ago, though he had been staying in Bengaluru for a long time. The reason for his lack of awareness was, according to him, that there was hardly any interaction among Telugus in day-to-day lives. Therefore, any information about Telugus living in Bengaluru would be difficult to get. It is only through such interactions at the personnel level that one would gain knowledge about different activities among Telugus. Unlike Tamils, Telugus hardly have any get-together.

Finally, we asked them whether they felt closer to Telugus than they did when they were in Andhra Pradesh.

Table 7.17 Feeling of closeness to Telugus

Do you now feel closer to Telugus than you did earlier when you came to Bengaluru?	Number	Percentage
(A) Yes. I feel much closer	95	79.17
(B) It is difficult to answer	8	6. 67
C) No. No change in my attitude towards other Telugus	17	14.16
Total	**120**	**100**

It is as though the feeling of being closer to Telugus is 'natural' and any question on this count is considered irrelevant. A significant number of respondents (95) have said that they now feel closer to other Telugus than they did earlier when they came to Bengaluru. The extent to which one feels closer to the member of one's 'own' group and the intensity with which one feels it perhaps depends on how unfamiliar the 'new place' is, in this case Bengaluru. If the majority of people feel closer to Telugus even in a place like Bengaluru that is not very far from Andhra Pradesh, one can imagine the condition of people living in the North-East, for example.

Contribution of this work to the existing body of knowledge

It has been our endeavour to make a modest addition to the existing literature that seeks to engage itself with a critical understanding of the relationship between modernization and ethnicity which was tended to be viewed rather uncritically. Major theoretical perspectives emanating from the works of Marx, Durkheim and Max Weber, for example, seek to posit a unilinear relationship between the two. Modernization (though viewed differently by them) would strike at the very root of ethnicity gradually resulting in the emasculation of ethnic identities. Popular assumptions too subscribe to this view, but the fact is it has not happened. The power of ethnic identities has proved to be irresistible.

Therefore, a number of scholars have begun to interrogate the relationship between modernization and ethnicity. They perceive a problematical and multidimensional relationship between the two. Our study constitutes an intervention in this debate and indicates the possibility of coexistence of modernity with ethnicity. One can also speak in terms of compartmentalization.

Evidently, the promise of modernity has proved to be a little exaggerated. When modernity appeared on the scene, it was celebrated. It privileged reason over faith, optimism over pessimism and knowledge over ignorance. It was expected to free us from the shackles of ignorance and irrationality enforced by tradition. Ethnicity was supposed to be one such shackle, being the embodiment of 'irrationality'. Clearly modernity has not displaced ethnicity. Our study provides further empirical evidence to this. Ethnic and communitarian identities have not withered away, because they are primordial, having ineffable and affective significance or because they have not been allowed to die a natural death given the desire of prominent political leaders of ethnic groups to utilize the obvious advantages attached to nurturing and maintaining ethnics identities in the socio-political context. Ethnic identities are being used as an instrument to achieve socioeconomic and political objectives, many of which are, paradoxically, specific to the 'modern' world. Whatever it may be, the fact remains, as our study shows, that modernity and ethnicity coexist.

This would also make us reflect on the larger issue of nation-state formation, though it has not been our direct concern in this work. What model of the 'nation-state' is to be followed is the question that arises as a byproduct of this work. Respect for cultural diversities and federal polity should be an organic component of any such model. Any model that seeks to homogenize diversities would fail because they continue to claim their cultural and ideological/political space.

Conclusion

As we have noted at the outset we have been fundamentally attracted towards the spectacular instances of resurgence of ethnicity both in the traditional and the so-called modern and advanced countries. Ethnic and communitarian identities have evidently become stronger than even before despite the inexorable process of modernization that was supposed to have a struck a blow to the 'primordial' identities. That is the implication one derives from the dominant theoretical perspectives (of Marx, Durkheim and Weber). Ethnicity would inevitably give way to the class consciousness, as Marx would argue. Or the movement from mechanical solidarity to the organic solidarity would privilege individual consciousness over collective conscience thereby implying that ethnic identities would lose their significance. The processes of secularization and rationalization would strike at the very root of ethnic conscience, as Max Weber would contend.

But today we are witnessing the growing salience of ethnicity in both traditional and the so-called modern societies. One can rationalize the salience of ethnicity, if one likes to, in terms of inadequate modernization in the former, but how would one do so in the case of modern and advanced societies? Evidently, the promise made by modernity – a product of Enlightenment that privileged reason over faith, knowledge over ignorance, optimism over pessimism – has not been fulfilled.. It was celebrated as a new possibility, as a new hope. It was expected to free us from all kinds of shackles. Ethnicity was supposed to be one such shackle. Evidently it has not happened.

This is what we wanted to know. Whether the same pattern is reproduced in the context of Telugus in Bengaluru is the central problem that we have tried to explore. More specifically, whether people who demonstrate attributes of modern consciousness also demonstrate attributes of ethnic consciousness. This would tell us whether modernization coexists with ethnic consciousness among Telugus in Bengaluru. We have sought to make one point quite clear. The absence of ethnic assertions and/or ethnic conflicts should not be taken to mean the absence of ethnic consciousness. The latter can exist even in the absence of the former. One need not wait for a conflict to erupt before exploring the consciousness that gives rise to such conflicts.

To do this, we had to gain conceptual clarity about modernity and ethnicity. We have, therefore, involved ourselves in a sustained engagement with these supposedly theoretically loose and methodologically unwieldy terms. Having done that, we have proceeded to examine the considerable body of literature that looks at the relationship between modernization and ethnicity (though not directly all the time). For the purpose of greater analytical clarity, we have divided the literature into theories of decline and theories of persistence; The former is subdivided into Marxist expectancy and liberal expectancy. In essence they argue in terms of decline of ethnicity. Reasons could differ depending on the ideological position they take. The latter would argue in terms of the persistence and in fact of resurgence of ethnicity. A review of the theories of persistence would give us, broadly, the following reasons for the persistence of ethnicity.

One of the important reasons for growing ethnic conflicts is said to be the model of the nation-state developed in Europe and spread through the entire world (apart from the process of modernization). It has been observed that this model has been found to be deficient in terms of satisfactorily accommodating numerous ethnic groups within its hold. Subordinate ethnic groups would not like to identify themselves with the state in which they live. They constantly endeavour to gain greater recognition, equality or autonomy within the framework of an existing territorial state or for independence from such a state.

This gives rise to numerous ethnic conflicts between the dominant ethnic groups who are in full control of the state and subordinate ethnic groups trying to gain more control over the state or to carve out a separate state of their own.

Such conflicts could be noticed in Europe too; they occurred in the aftermath of decolonization during the 1960s within the successor states of the European empires in Africa and Asia. We have also witnessed the re-emergence of ethnic conflicts as a result of the dissolution of the erstwhile Soviet Union and the Yugoslavia Federation in the early 1990s.

The second reason is associated with growing ethnic turbulence is the competition over declining socioeconomic resources. Whatever resources available, they are appropriated by the dominant ethnic group in a more effective way than the subordinate ethnic groups, leading to glaring inequalities. These growing inequalities have recently been aggravated by the process of globalization and the privatization of production activities. There has been a process of degradation of the socioeconomic reality of subordinate ethnic groups. And members of these groups have begun to realize that unless they stay together and fight for resources, they will not be able to gain anything. This leads to a great competition among ethnic group for the limited resources. Why should this fight assume an ethnic shape? As Daniel Bell suggests an ethnic group successfully combines an affective tie with an instrumental one. Mobilization along ethnic lines has been proven to be very effective in competing successfully for the resources. The fascinating story of Mizoram from a small district in the state of Assam into a full-fledged state of Mizoram reveals quite clearly that ethnicity could be mobilized successfully to gain access to political and economic resources.

Third, the very logic of modernization reaffirms the need for an identity. Modernization through its thrust on homogenization seeks to subvert everything that does not fit into its framework. It ridicules and castigates and undermines all other social and ethic cohesions and imposes its globalizing will and power on all others. It is the first claim to universality that leaves no one out of its domain. There is only one legitimate structure of power, morality and truth. All others are invalid.

The end result of this kind of worldview is that it creates a sense of rootlessness among people who get dragged, willingly or unwillingly, into the process of modernization. The 'authentic' identity that they have been nurturing all along stands diminished and discredited in the face of modernization. This creates a sense of restlessness and rootlessness leading to the inexorable process of searching for one's roots. This is where ethnicity steps in comforting the bruised psyche by providing authentic identity. Thus, modernization ironically reasserts and consolidates ethnicity.

Last, referring specifically to the Indian context, the inauguration of 'mass politics' has enhanced the significance of groups. Certain fundamental rights, introduction of adult suffrage and legal rights and consequent democratization have encouraged participation of a large number of people to take more active interest in their polity. In a democracy physical numbers matter the most. It has been noticed that ideology and party programmes alone are not sufficient to mobilize physical numbers in an electoral context. By harping on the group identity (ethnic identity) it has been observed that dominant elites in every ethnic group have been able to mobilize people along their side. Ethnicity has proven itself to be one such effective mobilize tool.

When M. N. Srinivas referred to the growing importance of caste in Indian politics in 1952, very few took him seriously. Subsequent elections reaffirmed the role played by caste in Indian politics. The Backward Classes Movement in Tamil Nadu in 1920s and more recently in the North India, especially Bihar and UP, are sharp pointers in this regard. Caste has been used as a very powerful mobilizing tool in India. Ethnic politics has become an incontrovertible political fact.

Let us turn to the place which we have chosen – Bengaluru. It must be stated quite clearly that choosing Bengaluru for our study purposes does not allude to or confirm the presence ethnic conflicts between Telugus and Kannadigas. Our attempt is essentially to understand whether modernization has led to the disappearance of ethnic consciousness: our findings suggest that it has not done so. It has been observed that ethnic consciousness may or may not lead to ethnic conflicts. Whether ethnic consciousness concretizes itself in terms of ethnic conflicts and, if so, at what time, would depend on historical and contextual factors. Absence of an ethnic conflict does not necessarily indicate absence of ethnic consciousness.

Ethnic conflicts do not become full-blown but usually go through a period of incubation. In Bengaluru also one does not witness any ethnic upheaval as much. However, one does not fail to notice certain amount of ethnic restlessness among Telugus. As their responses to our queries indicate, this has been caused by perceived discrimination against Telugus (as revealed in caste studies), the failure of democratic mechanism for negotiation or power-sharing between ethnic political actors, the emergence of essentialist ethnic ideologies and rigid and unaccommodating ethnic politics and the absence of prominent cultural space for Telugus.

It is with the objective of finding out whether the Telugu identity (ethnic identity) has become stronger even in the face of modernization that we have chosen Bengaluru. The logic underlying the choice of this city is that the prevailing cosmopolitan culture is supposed to have made deep inroads into the collective psyche and life of the residents of Bengaluru.

As it must have been noticed, our interest is with only those who have exhibited modern attributes such as readiness to face new experiences, preference for democracy, orientation towards present and/or future, respect for efficiency and emphasis on dignity. Responses only from these people have been sought in relation to their attitudes towards ethnicity. Systematic data from these responses only would help us make an enquiry into the problem as so whether modernization necessarily leads to the erasure of ethnic consciousness.

As far as our basic problem, that is, modernization, does not lead to the weakening of ethnic consciousness is concerned, a careful perusal of the responses to our questions and also cases studies would tell us that it has clearly not done so. Majority of respondents (more than 90 out of 120) have scored a mean score more than 2, which demonstrates that they think along ethnic lines. Although they think along modern lines, when it comes to the question of expression of ethnicity, one notices their continued ethnic consciousness.

Location of our study in the larger context

A look at the above findings and also our case studies would enable us to locate our study in the larger context of how modernity has found itself incapable of weakening ethnic and community identities. The promise of modernity has proved to be a little exaggerated one. The power of identity has proved to be intractable. Identities persist became they have tremendous emotional significance for the people or because these identities have emerged as powerful instruments that are used to achieve political and socioeconomic objectives. Whatever it is, our study provides empirical evidence for the possibility of coexistence of modernity and ethnicity. Modernity instead of looking down upon identity needs would do well to engage itself in a creative dialogue with identity.

This would also lead us to briefly reflect on the very question of nation-state formation, which is viewed largely as a modern process. Although this issue has not been our main concern in this work, it should be possible to make a brief reference here. The concept of nation-state transplanted here from Europe has not proved to be a tenable and sustainable doctrine. Within Europe itself, as T. K. Oommen would argue, it has largely remained a myth. There have been different nations within the Europe itself, an empirical reality that has been conveniently pushed under the carpet. One could usefully speak in terms of multiple nations within a State itself. What should remain a common bond is the citizenship. The hegemonic concept of the nation-state would find itself incapable of being accepted by the subordinate groups who feel left out of the system.

The efforts being made at present, in the name of cultural nationalism, to homogenize cultural diversities would do immense conceptual and physical violence to our body politic and society. Such efforts betray an astounding ignorance of our history and culture.

Culture is an inclusive term and the reduction of it to religion would be untenable.

In our view what needs to be privileged is the respect for cultural diversities and the federal polity. It is only by privileging these two can a sense of belonging be instilled in different ethnic groups of population. Every group would like to have its own ideological and political space. Competent claims of different groups can meaningfully be accommodated within the framework of federal polity and cultural diversities. Any tendency in the name of modernity to homogenize cultural diversities and to make any one model hegemonic would make the very project of modernity a problematic proposition.

REFERENCES

Barth, F. (ed.). 1969. *Ethnic Groups and Boundaries: The Social Organization of Culture Difference*. London: Allen and Unwin.

Bell, B. 1975. Ethnicity and social change. In N. Glazer & D. P. Moynihan (eds), *Ethnicity: Theory and Experience* (pp.141-174). Cambridge, MA: Harvard University Press.

Bendix R. 1964. *Nation-building and Citizenship: Studies of Our Changing Social Order*. New York: Wiley.

Black, C. E. 1966. *The Dynamics of Modernization: A Study in Comparative History*. New York: Harper and Row.

Brass, P. 1974. *Language, Religion and Politics in North India*. London: Cambridge University Press.

———. 1991. *Ethnicity and Nationalism: Theory and Comparison*. New Delhi: Sage.

Bromley, Y. 1974. The term ethnos and its definition. In Y. Brumley (ed.), *Soviet Ethnology and Anthropology Today*. The Hague: Manton.

Cohen, A. 1974. The lesson of ethnicity. In A. Cohen (ed.), *Urban Ethnicity* (ASA Monograph 12, pp. 9–14). London: Tavistock.

Durkheim, E. 1964. *The Division of Labour in Society*. New York: Free Press.

Geertz, C. 1975. Thick description: Towards an interpretive theory of culture. In C. Geertz (ed.), *The Interpretation of Culture* (pp 78-85). London: Hutchinson.

Giddens, A. 1990. *The Consequences of Modernity*. Cambridge, MA: Polity.

Glazer, N. & Moynihan D. P. 1963. *Beyond the Melting Pot: The Negroes, Puerto Ricans, Jews, Italians and Irish of New York*. Cambridge, MA: MIT Press. (Revised 1970)

Glazer, N. & Moynihan, D. P. (eds). 1976. *Ethnicity: Theory and Experience*. Cambridge, MA: Harvard University Press.

Habermas, J. 1987. *The Philosophical Discourse of Modernity* (trans. F. Lawrence). Cambridge, MA: MIT Press.

Hector, M. 1975. *Internal Colonialism: The Celtic Fringe in British National Development, 1536–1996*. London: Routeldge and Kegan Paul.

Hoselitz, B. 1960. *Sociological Aspects of Economic Growth*. New York: Free Press.

Inkeles, A. 1966. The modernization of man. In M. Weiner (ed.), *Modernization: The Dynamics of Growth* (pp. 57-73). New York: Basic Books.

Issacs, H. 1975. Basic group identity: The ideals of the tribe. In N. Glazer & D. P. Moynihan (eds), *Ethnicity: Theory and Experience* (pp. 29-52). Cambridge, MA: Harvard University Press.

Lerner, D. 1958. *The Passing of Traditional Society*. New York: Free Press.

Levi, M. J. 1966. *Modernization and the Structure of Societies* (Vol. 1 & 2). Princeton, NJ: Princeton University Press.

Marx K. 1859. *Contribution to the Critique of Political Economy*. Moscow: Progress Publishers.

Parsons, T. 1971. *The System of Modern Society*. Englewood Cliffs, NJ: Prentice Hall.

Rex, J. 1970. *Race Relations in Sociological Theory*. New York: Schachess.

Roosens, E. E. 1989. *Creating Ethnicity*. London: Sage.

Shils, E. 1961. *The Intellectual between Tradition and Modernity: The Indian Situation*. The Hague: Mouton and Co.

Smelser, N. J. 1969. Mechanism of change and adjustment to change. In T. Burns (ed.), *Industrial Man* (pp 86-91). Harmondsworth, UK: Penguin.

Smith, A. D. 1981. *The Ethnic Revival*. Cambridge, UK: Cambridge University Press.

Srinivas, M. N. 1996. *Indian Society through Personnel Writings*. New Delhi: Oxford University Press.

Weber, M. 1922. *Economy and Society*. Los Angeles: University of California Press.

———, 1904–1905. *The Protestant Ethics and the Spirit of Capitalism* (trans. T. Parson). London: Routledge.

8

Interrogating development

Any book of this kind is usually, and perhaps rightly so, expected to diagnose the 'problem' and throw up 'solutions'. I would however plead guilty for being unable to do so. What I would, however, attempt to do is problematize the very notion of development. How does one look at development? What are the multiple understandings of development that one can engage oneself with and the problematics that are associated with each understanding? This should not be taken to mean that the other idea, that is, peace, is completely free from problematics. Although it too is a problematical notion, there appears to be a certain amount of agreement about what peace means. It is usually defined as the absence of insurgent and militant activities especially in the context of the North-East. I would, however, not proceed further on this. I would also not dwell on the relationship between peace and development because that would mean getting into the 'chicken and egg quandary'. Which comes first? Peace or development? Some would argue that unless there is relative peace in the society, development would be difficult to achieve. Others, with equal stringency, take the position that unless there is development in the society in the first place, there would be no peace. It is indeed a very interesting dialectic, which I am not sure I am capable of dealing with. Since my interest is essentially theoretical and analytical, I would also not dwell on the situation in Mizoram (it would be beyond the scope of this chapter), except make a very preliminary and tentative comment at the end. In this chapter, it will be my modest endeavour to look at the problematics connected with the very notion of development.

In a popular perception, development has generally and uncritically been equated with economic growth. Development in this sense would mean higher GDP, national income, per capita income and so on. However, such a narrow understanding of development has been questioned. There is a need to have a more elaborate and comprehensive understanding of development, which I think is possible to obtain by taking a look at the rich sociological literature available to us.

The notion development has had a very rich and long background in sociological literature. It needs to be stated that by the time development began to make inroads into social science literature, there were certain others notions that were already in use to explain the transformations taking place in the European society (Bottomore 1962). One of those notions was social evolution, which was directly taken from the theories of biological evolution. Herbert Spencer, who was one of the greatest exponents of the idea of evolution, drew an analogy between biological organism and societies (this led him to draw an analogy between social evolution and biological evolution). He argued that our understanding of social evolution would be much better if one first acquired an understanding of how biological evolution proceeded, though in his account of social evolution he himself paid less attention to the more specific features of the biological evolution. The notion of evolution had its serious problematics that slowly undermined its usefulness as a category of the analysis of social transformations taking place. It would be misleading to draw an analogy between social evolution and biological evolution because man's social and cultural behaviour is essentially learned, whereas the behaviour of an organism is inborn.

Moreover, changes in culture and tradition are regulated by social actors, which is not the case with changes in biological organisms.

Then there was the idea of progress, which was in currency to describe transformations taking place. However, it fell into disrepute because of both intellectual and social factors. Intellectually, there was a growing attempt to make sociology a value-free science. Sociology needed to be concerned not with 'what ought to be' but with 'what is'. The function of sociology was to make an objective and scientific study of society. It was not to dabble in issues of improvement, progress and emancipation. The use of the notion of progress would have entailed engagement with the question of values, which did not fit into the framework of a value-free sociology. Socially, the idea of progress seemed a cruel joke in the context of growing poverty, glaring socioeconomic inequalities, devastation caused by nuclear wars and, more recently, increasingly visible pathological tendencies associated with the project of modernity.

The idea of development was believed to be eminently suitable to describe the changes taking in the societies. However, it has had an interesting trajectory that has not been free from problematics. In fact, there is considerable amount of disagreement over what constitutes development. It would indeed be an interesting exercise to engage ourselves with its multiple understandings. It is possible to look at development from three distinct perspectives (Portes 1988, pp. 171–211).

1. Development as social differentiation
2. Development as enactment of values
3. Development as freedom from dependency

Development as social differentiation

It was in the writings of evolutionary thinkers such as Auguste Comte, Herbert Spencer, Morgan and Durkheim that one found that development was essentially looked at a process of growing social differentiation (of which structural differentiation is one primary component) and functional specialization (Bogardus 1940). They essentially looked at societies as moving from simple, homogenous, undifferentiated state to complex, heterogeneous and differentiated social existence. For them this constituted the very process of development. Comte looked at the development of societies from the theological, through metaphysical and finally to the positive stage. This process of social differentiation was an integral part of the general societal development (Bogardus 1940). The movement of societies from the mechanical stage, characterized as it was by an undifferentiated structure of values, norms and positions, to the organic stage, characterized as it was by a growing differentiation of the same, constituted for Durkheim the very core of developmental process (Durkheim 1933).

It was Herbert Spencer who gave us a more elaborate and comprehensive account of the evolutionary process of development (Sztompka 1993, pp. 102–103). His argument is based on three fundamental assumptions. First, individuals are fundamentally unequal with respect to the genetic endowments, experiences, the environmental conditions in which they live and opportunities and deprivations they experience. This leads to an increasing differentiation of roles, functions, power, prestige and wealth. Second, and this is the logical extension of the first, unequal access to power and wealth gets multiplied and aggravated resulting in greater and cumulative strengthening of initial differentiation. Third, as people of similar positions tend to cohere, the society increasingly becomes differentiated into factions, classes and groups, and it becomes impossible for a return to take place to homogeneity. This mechanism leads to movement of societies from a simple stage through complex stage, then doubly complex societies up to civilization (the most developed states of societies).

This kind of understanding of development has certain serious problematics that need to be understood. First, it is too an abstract and a universal approach to be of any significant use in understanding any specific empirical situation. Difficulties would arise when one seeks to apply it in the context of any particular society. It would not really help us in understanding why transformations (the factors responsible for them) have taken place in certain societies and not in others. A sociological study of development would be weaker if it does not spell out the factors responsible for social transformations. Second, the evolutionary theories of development are gradualist in their orientation and would therefore fail to account for sudden occurrences, discontinuities and reversals. No societal transformation can be totally unilinear. They are bound to be continuities and discontinuities, sudden thrusts and convulsions, a point that has not been sufficiently appreciated in the evolutionary understanding of development.

Development as enactment of values

The second major way of approaching development is through explication of certain core values and attitudes. Here development implies the internalization of certain socio-psychological attributes. Development is there if these are present and it is not there when these attributes are absent.

Unlike the first approach that gives a descriptive account of development, the second approach, that is, development as enactment of values, is explanatory. It seeks to dwell upon the factors that cause development. The roots of this approach should be traced to Max Weber's thesis on *Protestant Ethics and the Spirit of Capitalism* (1958). Max Weber in what was then considered a brilliant though controversial account of the growth of capitalism dealt with the relationship between capitalism and the Protestant ethics. He sought to explain the growth of capitalism in terms of motivational structure provided by the Protestant sect. Apart from certain other factors such as rational law, rational accounting system, technology that played a major role in the growth of capitalism, the ethics provided the right motivational framework for generating a suitable behavioural and cultural environment (such as hard work, thrift as a noble goal, work is worship etc.) in which capitalism would grow. It must be stated quite clearly, contrary to popular perception, Max Weber never contended that the Protestant ethic was *the factor* for the growth of capitalism. It was only one of the factors responsible for its growth. His emphasis was on the notion of calling, predestination and 'select few' finally led to a strong motivation to work harder and become successful, virtues that were crucial for the development of capitalism.

Later on, more psychologically oriented theories of development, such as those of McClelland, Hagen and Alex Inkeles, dominated the discourse on development. They sought to explain development in terms of possession of certain psychological attributes. David McClelland was one of the first who dwelt at length on the need to acquire the required psychological attributes to achieve development (McClelland 1963). He essentially focused on what he called n-Ach (short name for need for achievement). He argued that this was a critical factor for development. He gathered both historical and empirical proof to defend his position. For example, he found that in Achievement scores obtained from content analysis of folk tales from preliterate societies correlated with the presence of some full-time entrepreneurs in the society. Similarly n Achievement scores obtained from teachers employed to teach children in 21 different societies in 1925 are positively correlated with the idea of economic growth in those societies between 1929 and 1950 (McClelland 1963, pp. 28–39).

There have been other attempts at spelling out attributes necessary for achieving development. One of such attempts was that of Alex Inkeles (1966, pp. 138–150). On the basis of a cross-cultural study of six developing countries (India, Pakistan, Nigeria, Israel, Argentina and Chile), he explicated nine attributes and values that characterize a modern man. They are readiness for new experience and openness to innovation, disposition to form and hold opinion, democratic orientation, planning habits, belief in human and personal efficacy, stress on personal and human dignity, faith in science and technology, belief that the world is calculable and belief in distributive justice.

There have been some attempts to engage in an empirical study using his understanding of modernity (Kumar 2006). However, this way of looking at development, it must be admitted, has certain serious limitations. First, by emphasizing only on socio-psychological attributes as components of development, it remains essentially individualistic and motivational in orientation. It tends to ignore the relevance of structural and cultural factors that play a role that is no less important in the process of development. The kind of negative role that social structural forms, for example, in India played reducing the momentum of development, if not completely blocking it, has been pointed out time and again. I am, however, aware of the powerful literature that has been produced seeking to look at other factors such as the impact of colonial rule blocking development in India (e.g. Desai 1948). Still others point to the adaptive nature of different structural forms like the caste system and argue that there is no evidence, historical or otherwise, to prove that they have blocked development (Singh 1973). The key point, however, is that one cannot completely ignore the importance and relevance of structural and cultural institutions present in the society for the process of development.

Second, some others would argue, as we will just see, this kind of approach remains completely oblivious of structural linkages that have existed between developed and undeveloped/underdeveloped countries. They argue that development in the West has taken place essentially because of their ability to exploit these linkages. They would further argue that if development is to take place in the poorer countries they have to break these linkages and 'go it alone'.

Development as freedom from dependency

Yet another way of defining development is in terms of achieving liberation or freedom from the structures of dependency that characterize the world capitalist system. This view has been taken by a very powerful literature that was developed on the basis of the Latin American experience and has come to be variously known as dependency theory, world systems theory or underdevelopment theory (Amin 1974, Baran 1973, Frank 1978, Wallerstein 1979). Although this body of thought has also been characterized as a neo-Marxist theory of development because of its privileging of the notions of exploitation and oppression, it must be understood that, unlike Marxists, they take the position that 'underdevelopment' and not 'development' is the direct result of the spread of international capitalism.

The essential arguments of the dependency theory are as follows:

1. Development and underdevelopment are aspects of the same economic process and the former has been able to occur only by increasing the latter.
2. It expresses itself strongly against the other theories of development mentioned above on the ground that they ignore the linkages that exist between the developed countries and the poorer countries. These linkages are effectively used by the developed world in extracting raw materials, cheap labour and appropriating the markets of poorer countries.
3. They argue that the existence of the world capitalist system means that the development potential of the underdeveloped countries is blocked.
4. The capitalist world system commenced when the Western nations developed trading links with non-European countries gradually incorporating the rest of the world.
5. The transnational companies are, in particular, regarded as the main agents of neocolonialism, in that they are a vital mechanism in the transfer of surplus from the periphery or semi-periphery to the centre.
6. The only hope for the underdeveloped countries is to severe links with the developed world and 'go it alone'. Immanuel Wallerstein, however, recognizes the fact that peaceful cutting of the links is not possible. Rather there should an organized protest and dissent to be able to assert their freedom and independence (Wallerstein 1979).

A careful reading of the dependency theory would reveal certain difficulties with this approach. First, the dependency theory does not have space for class and class struggle, which are crucial in bringing about social changes. Marxists have found it difficult to subscribe to what the dependency theorists argue (Leys 1980, Phillips 1977). The whole Marxist argument is based on the revolutionary role that class struggle plays in bringing about basic structural changes in the society. Ignoring such an important explanatory category would not find favour with the Marxists. Second, some others who are not Marxists would argue that contrary to what dependency theorists say growth rates in some parts of the Third World have been higher than in the developed countries (Warren 1973). An indigenous capitalist class is actively promoting innovation, accumulating capital, involving itself in manufacturing and so on. The growth is also reflected in areas like education, nutrition, health, mortality rates and housing. Their argument is based on the basic point put forward by the dependency theorists – the underdeveloped countries would continue to become poorer and poorer because of the structures of exploitation and subjugation over which the developed countries have complete control. Others arguing on the basis of empirical findings say that some countries have remained underdeveloped not because they have become part of the world capitalist system but because they have remained outside it. For example, Latin America did not develop not because it was incorporated into the world capitalist system but because it did not have proper trading links with Europe (Platt 1980). Third, still others would argue that the dependency theorists completely neglect the relevance of local structures and cultural patterns in encouraging or discouraging the developmental process (Ray 1973).

Thus, as mentioned at the outset, my attempt has been quite modest in the sense that I have only tried to engage myself briefly with multiple understandings of development with the intention of developing certain sensitivity to each of them and becoming clearer about what we mean by development. Whereas the first understanding, that is, development as social differentiation, found a powerful expression in the writings of evolutionary thinkers, it does not mean much in the present-day context, as it is essentially *descriptive* in nature and does not help us in ensuring development. The other two understandings of development, that is, development as enactment of values and freedom from dependency, are essentially *explanatory* in the sense that they tell us, though they too have some problems, what development is and what causes it.

In the context of the North-East in general and Mizoram in particular, I would take the position that development needs to be understood in terms of achieving freedom from dependence on the 'mainstream' India. By saying so, I am trying to contextualize the powerful ideas of the dependency theory (which were, however, about the world capitalist system in general). There is an urgent need to think of a developmental model that takes into account locally available resources and needs of people. Only in that way would the developmental process be not only sustainable but also reduce dependence on the 'dominant' mainstream. It is for the economists, sociologists, political scientists and other concerned intellectuals to conceptualize through a dialogic process such a model of development.

REFERENCES

Amin, S. 1974. Accumulation and development: A theoretical model. *Review of African Political Economy*, 1, 9–26.

Baran, P. 1973. *The Political Economy of Growth*. Harmondsworth, UK: Penguin.

Bogardus, C. 1940. *The Development of Social Thought*. New York: Longman.

Bottomore, T. B. 1962. *Sociology: A Guide to Problems and Literature*. London: Allen and Unwin.

Desai, A. R. 1948. *Social Background of Indian Nationalism*. Bombay: Popular Publishers

Durkheim, E. 1933. *On the Division of Labour in Society*. New York: Macmillan.

Frank, A. G. 1978. *Dependent Accumulation and Underdevelopment*. London: Macmillan.

Inkeles, A. 1966. The modernisation of man. In M. Weiner (ed.), *Modernisation: The Dynamics of Growth* (pp. 138–150). New York: Basic Books.

Kumar, D. V. 2006. *Modernisation and Ethnicity*. New Delhi: Mittal Publications.

Leys, C. 1980. Kenya: What does 'dependency' explain? *Review of African Political Economy*, 17, 108–113.

McClelland, D. C. 1963. The impulse of modernisation. In M. Weiner (ed.), *Modernisation: The Dynamics of Growth* (pp. 28–39). New York: Basic Books.

Phillips, A. 1977. The concept of development. *Review of African Political Economy*, 8, 7–20.

Platt, D. C. M. 1980. Dependency in nineteenth-century America: An historian objects. *Latin American Research Review*, 15(1), 147–149.

Portes, A. 1988. On the sociology of national development: Theories and issues. In R. Pandey (ed.), *Modernisation and Social Change* (pp. 171–211). New Delhi: Criterion Publications.

Ray, D. 1973. The dependency model of Latin American underdevelopment: Three basic fallacies. *Journal of Inter-American Studies*, 15(1), 4–20.

Singh, Y. 1973. *Modernisation of Indian Tradition (A Systemic Study of Social Change)*. Faridabad, Haryana, India: Thomson.

Sztompka, P. 1993. *The Sociology of Social Change*. Oxford, UK: Blackwell.

Wallerstein, I. 1979. *The Capitalist World Economy*. Cambridge, UK: Cambridge University press

Warren, B. 1973. Imperialism and capitalist industrialisation. *New Left Review*, 80, 3–44.

Weber, M. 1958. *The Protestant Ethic and the Spirit of Capitalism*. London: Allen and Unwin.

9

Tribal development

Issues, movements and interventions

The issue of tribal development has become salient in the context of the democratic and liberal framework that has been adopted in India. The legitimacy of a democratic framework depends to a great extent on its ability to meet the needs and aspirations of the most submerged, exploited and neglected sections of the society. Lack of concern for these sections would erode the very moral legitimacy that such a framework claims to possess. Needless to add, tribes constitute such a section of the society. They occupy the lowest rungs of social, economic and political structure of the society. Historically they suffered at the hands of the dominant sections of the society. Even from the State, whether we are talking about the pre-colonial, colonial or postcolonial one, tribals have not received the kind of attention that they always deserved or even demanded.

The constitution-makers deeply conscious of the fact that there were certain sections or groups that have been subjected to historical neglect and deprivation and therefore needed to be uplifted conceived of several measures and steps. Apart from the fundamental rights that were granted to everybody, certain specific steps were initiated for the improvement of conditions of tribal groups. The inclusion of the Sixth Schedule of the Constitution that provides for greater political autonomy for the tribals in the North-East is a case in point. The provision of a Special Commissioner to look into the developmental needs and requirements of people belonging to the Scheduled Castes and Scheduled Tribes is another. The policy of reservation in educational and employment sectors is yet another important step in that direction. Apart from the above, successive governments conceived and executed different developmental programmes and policies whose main focus is on the advancement of the conditions of the tribals. Whether all of the above has had any positive effect on the status of tribals is a moot question. In fact, the very model of development that has been initiated for tribals in general and tribal communities in the North-East in particular has been severely criticized (Pathy 1998). It has been said that the developmental model followed in India with its hegemonizing and homogenizing logic subverts the traditions and identity of tribals. It has led to the dispossession of tribals of their traditional sources of livelihood. It has made them vulnerable to exploitation from outsiders in the name of development. The construction of high dams and projects, again in the name of development, has led to their displacement and ecological destruction. It has done physical, psychological and conceptual violence.

We, therefore, need to critically interrogate the issues concerning their development. We will also deal with the various tribal movements, which we like to emphasize, have emerged essentially due to an inadequate appreciation of issues relating to their development. At the end, we look at some of the meaningful interventions that should be made with utmost seriousness. Before we do so, we need to look at the geographical distribution of tribals and the development programmes undertaken during the plan period so far in order to gain a general appreciation of their spread and the present status.

Although tribals are distributed all over the country, one can identify a few concentration points. Roy Burman (1972) and Vidyarthi

(1977) have suggested a more or less identical six-fold classification on the basis of regional distribution of the tribal population:

(1) **North-eastern region:** In states like Manipur, Arunachal Pradesh, Nagaland, Assam, Mizoram and Meghalaya live tribes like Abor, Garo, Khasi, Mizo, Naga, Mismi, who mostly belong to the Mongolian racial stock.

(2) **Himalayan region:** In the sub-Himalayan regions covering parts of North Bengal, Uttar Pradesh and Himachal Pradesh live tribes like Lepcha and Rabha mostly belonging to Mongolian racial group.

(3) **Central India region:** In older hills and Chota Nagpur Plateau, along the dividing lines between Peninsular India and the Indo-Gangetic basin live many tribal communities like the Bhumij, Gond, Ho, Oraon, Munda, Santhal, covering the states of Bihar, Orissa, Madhya Pradesh and West Bengal and mostly belonging to Proto-Australoid racial stock.

(4) **Western India region**: Covering the states like Rajasthan, Maharashtra, Gujarat, Goa, Dadra and Nagar Haveli live a number of tribal communities, the most important of them being the Bhil racially belonging to the Proto-Australoid group.

(5) **Southern India region:** Covering the states of Karnataka, Andhra Pradesh, Tamil Nadu and Kerala, in the Nilgiri Hills and converging lines of the Ghats live the Chenchu, Kadar, Toda etc. having Negrito, Caucasoid, Proto-Australoid or mixed physical features.

(6) **Island region:** Covering Andaman, Nicobar and Lakshadweep Islands live a number of small tribes like Andamanese and Orge.

If one looks at the distribution of tribals a little more closely, an interesting feature emerges. In some states they constitute an overwhelming proportion of their population, whereas in the whole country they form an insignificant percentage of population. For example, tribals constitute 83.99 per cent of population in Nagaland but only 1.26 per cent of the total tribal population of India. Similarly in Mizoram they constitute 93.55 per cent of population but only 0.89 per cent of the total tribal population of India (Chaudhuri 1982, p. xviii). This clearly indicates that in a number of states or union territories the tribals constitute the bulk of the population, whereas in others they are outnumbered by non-tribals. This type of demographic variation is, however, bound to affect the socioeconomic, political and cultural processes among tribes.

If one looks at the economic activities that tribals are engaged in, one can broadly categorize them as food gathering (including hunting and fishing), pastoral, shifting hill cultivation, settled agriculture, handicrafts, trade and commerce, labour work, including agriculture and industry.

For example, it is well known that the tribes of the North-East India mostly follow the shifting cultivation and those of Central and Western India follow settled agriculture and rudimentary trade and commerce. A study on the different tribal communities indicates that 139 communities depend on settled cultivation, 84 on shifting cultivation, 11 on terrace cultivation, 39 on collection, 19 on hunting, 7 on fishing, 15 on animal husbandry, 49 on handicrafts, 7 on trade and commerce and 40 on labour work primarily (Danda 1973, p. 42)

However, it needs to be mentioned that these statistics only reveal the predominant activities that they are engaged in. Most of them are engaged in a multiplicity of occupations, and development programmes need to take account of this fact.

Tribal development: meaning and scope

It may be relevant to get some idea about how anthropologists view development in general and tribal development in particular. Till some time back, growth and development were used interchangeably. It is only in the recent past that development has begun to be used in a qualitative sense. Earlier the two terms were used to refer to quantitative and mostly economic aspects. Now development is used to refer to social, cultural, economic and other aspects of life. According to Belshaw, for example, 'Sociologically speaking, development should be looked upon as an organized activity with the aim of satisfying certain basic needs and to psychologically orient the tribals to adopt new skills, attitudes and lifestyles, so that they build up the inner strength and appropriate social and cultural infrastructure to stand the pressure of the new situations and accrue benefits from new programmes and maintain high level' (Belshaw 1972, p. 44). In a later article, he has considered development as a positive change and observed, 'Development presents an increase in the capacities of a society to organize for its own objectives and to carry out its programmes more efficiently' (Belshaw 1977, p. 31)

Vidyarthi observes that development means growth and change, which includes both material and human – sociocultural factors that are an integral part of the dynamics of growth. He felt, 'While striving for the development of a group or an area, due emphasis has to be given to their traditional values and historical experiences' (1981, p. 96). In fact, economists like Schumacher also observe development does not start with goods; it starts with people and their education, organization and discipline. Some people take a more comprehensive view of tribal development and in fact go on to elucidate the specific components of the same. For example, to Roy Burman (1986) development activities, particularly in the context of tribals, should be concerned with satisfaction of minimum needs, control and management of productive resources, employment optimization, broad-based participation of the population in development process and socio-cultural and political aspects of national integration (1986, p. 133).

Coming to upliftment of tribals and enhancing the quality of their life and their absorption into mainstream society, a number of development programmes have been undertaken. In the first plan, various programmes were initiated with specific reference to health and communication mostly as part of community development programmes. In the second plan, 43 special multipurpose Tribal Blocks were set up for an integrated Tribal Development Programme. They came to be known as Tribal Development Blocks in the third period, and major emphasis was given to education in addition to health, agriculture, communication and housing programmes. By the end of the fourth plan, 43 per cent of the tribal population was covered in 504 Tribal Development Blocks. In this period a number of special programmes were initiated for the poorer families or small marginal farmers. Special attention was directed to the individual families during this period in addition to area-based programmes. It was only in the fifth plan a landmark event happened. For the first time, the concept of sub-plan for the tribal region of a state within the overall framework of the state plan was initiated. The tribal sub-plan approach initiated in the fifth plan continued in the sixth plan. The main objective was to narrow the gap between the level of development of tribal areas and others and to improve the quality of life of the tribal people. To achieve this, different economic programmes and protective measures having a bearing on their employment, education and health services were initiated.

Despite the various development programmes the conditions of tribals continue to remain quite unsatisfactory. Poverty still remains a major issue calling for serious attention from development agencies. Health, education, infrastructural and communication facilities are still in a rudimentary state. One more issue that has become extremely critical in the contemporary tribal world is the issue of identity. One notices a heightened sense of ethnic/cultural consciousness among tribals. Exploitation from outsiders continues unabated. The so-called development programmes, instead of improving the conditions, have actually worsened them. For example, the establishment of big dams and projects ostensibly for the purpose of facilitating development has actually dispossessed tribals of their control over the forests (which constituted the secondary source of livelihood) and led to further economic impoverishment. On the basis of empirical examination, one tends to conclude that development programmes have not benefited the tribal communities; sometimes development had been at the cost of tribal interests. Because of the skewed development process, one notices aggravation of socioeconomic inequalities among tribals themselves. The emergence of elites among tribals is illustrative of this.

Despite so much emphasis being given to the development of tribals nothing much significant seems to have happened that speaks for improved living conditions of tribals. In fact, the socio-economic conditions have worsened due to the skewed development process. This is reflected in a number of scholarly studies conducted on tribal development in India (Bose et al. 1990, Imchen 1990, Mahapatra 1972, Pathy 1998, Roy Burman 1986, Singh 2002, Sinha 2002, Thakur 2001, Vidyarthi 1981, to mention a few)

This is because the basic issues concerning tribal development have not been properly appreciated. Let us proceed to gain an appreciation of some of these issues.

Issues in tribal development

If one makes a critical and objective analysis of tribal development, the following issues would come to light:

1. Policies and programmes have been formulated without taking into account the social and cultural aspects of tribal population. As a result, development process has been seen as more of an imposition rather than as a process intimately connected to their life process. Values, beliefs, personality traits and sociopolitical disposition of the natives have been ignored (Imchen 1990). A proper and meaningful development process needs to take the above into account.
2. The whole development process has been initiated without paying serious attention to the needs and resource base of the tribals (Chaudhuri 1982, p. xviii). There has been excessive focus on industrialization, exploitation of mineral and forest resources, development of energy services such as thermal or atomic and change from shifting cultivation to settled agriculture and so on without adequately appreciating the requirements, needs and the resource structure of tribals. The development process should not result in the loss of traditional customary rights of tribals over productive resources. The tribals believe in the name of development their exploitation at the hands of outsiders has increased. Outsiders come, dispossess them of their own resources and gain control over the same.

3. There has been an exclusive emphasis on the development of quantitative aspects. The qualitative aspects such as health and education are not given sufficient importance. All over the world social indicators of development have acquired saliency, and the same should be extended to the issue of development among tribals.

4. The issue of participation of tribals at every stage of development process, from the stage of conceptualization to that of implementation, has not been properly emphasized. Unless tribals for whom tribal development programmes are meant are involved at every stage of the process, it would not be meaningful.

5. Development should help in the elimination or at least reduction of various processes of domination and cultural hegemony of ruling classes and equalization of distribution of development benefits. However, what one notices is exactly the opposite of what is mentioned above. Development measures have led to the emergence of elites and the strengthening of dominant and hegemonic structures in the tribal society. Owners of capital have become the agents and beneficiaries of development. As a result, the socioeconomic inequalities have become more pervasive among tribals (Imchen 1990).

6. Development programmes should have an adequate appreciation of variation in development from region to region and tribe to tribe. Some tribes have reached a higher stage of development than others. Different policies and programmes need to be formulated depending on the region and tribe.

7. Administrative structures that are entrusted with the responsibility of ensuring development should be made more responsive and receptive to the needs and aspirations of tribals.

8. Another issue that is intrinsically connected to the issue of development is cultural identity. The dialectic between

culture and development needs to be examined thoroughly. There is a predominant perception among tribals that developmental programmes and activities have led to the erosion of their cultural practices and traditions and the imposition of 'outside' cultures upon them. As a result, their 'identity' is in danger. Almost all tribal groups in North-East India entertain such a perception.

Tribal movements

Failure to adequately appreciate the issues mentioned above, as it has often been contended, has led to the emergence of different tribal movements at different points of time. There have been a number of tribal movements in India. For example, Kathleen Gough (1979) has recorded nearly 77 tribal uprisings. Similarly V. Raghavaiah (1979) after a meticulous survey of the tribal revolts between 1718 and 1971 informs that as many as 78 tribal revolts took place during this period. Tribal movements have been the subject of many scholarly studies (Alam 1989; Arnold 1982; Bhattacharjee 1989; Dutta 1985; Duyker 1987; Guha 1989a, 1989b; Hussain 1987; Karna 1998; Paul 1989; R. Guha 1983; Rotter-Hogan 1982; Sengupta 1980; Sharma 1986; Singh 1982, 1983a, 1983b; Weiner 1978)

The emergence of various tribal movements in the country can be attributed to the failure on the part of the British Colonial administration and later the Indian and different state governments to adequately appreciate the aforementioned issues. These movements are an expression of anger of tribals to the continued state of negligence to which they are subjected.

Before we deal with specific reasons for the emergence of tribal movements, it may be pertinent to have a preliminary idea of what a social movement is.

The term 'movement' acquired prominence sometime in the nineteenth century. It was in the wake of industrialization and French Revolution that it became the topic of study and analysis by social thinkers. Perhaps the first historian to write about social movements was Lorenz Von Stein, a Danish historian. In his book, *The History of Social Movement in France between 1789–1850* (cited in

Deniroff 1974, p. 1), he defines a social movement as 'people joined together in order to change conditions in society'.

Attempting conceptually a more rigorous definition, T. K. Oommen says, 'A social movement means those purposive mobilizations of people informed of an ideology to promote changes in any direction using any means violent or non-violent and functioning at least in an elementary organizational framework. Inevitably, social movement implies a series of interactions between two or more contending social groups to gain or deny critical societal resources – wealth, power and privilege' (1981, p. 1).

He has classified social movements into three broad typologies (1981, p. 2)

a. Primordial collectivities pursuing symbolic goals (e.g. reform movements, conversion movement for linguistic recognition etc.)
b. Civil collectivities pursuing instrumental goals (e.g. students' movement, peasant and youth movements etc.)
c. Primordial collectivities pursuing instrumental goals (e.g. caste movements for political and economic power, linguistic and tribal movement for separate statehood and political autonomy or sovereign state respectively etc.)

M. S. A. Rao regards collective mobilization, orientation to change and ideology as constituting three crucial features of a social movement (1979, p. 16). The involvement of a collective, be it caste, tribe or class, is the first critical feature of a social movement. Second, every social movement is supposed to bring about a 'desired' state of affairs. That is, it is oriented towards change, either partial or total in the existing system of relationship, values and norms. Third, what provides content to a social movement is the ideology. A social movement bereft of any ideology tends to degenerate into an isolated event.

Rao has classified social movements into four general types (1979, p. 3)

a. Depending on the consequences of a movement, they can be reformative, transformative and revolutionary.

b. Based on the focus of movement, they can be religious, caste, workers, peasants, tribals, women and student movement.

c. Based on the scale and spatial spread of movement, it can be all-India, regional and local.

d. Based on the issue of interests such as women liberation movements etc.

Having hopefully acquired some understanding of social movements and their classification, let us proceed to deal with the specific factors responsible for the emergence of tribal movements at different points of time in the history of India.

In an analytically sound review of tribal solidarity movements in India, Surajit Sinha (2002) looks at the tribal solidarity movements in India from the perspective of space and time. Spatially, solidarity movements range from tribes who are least integrated to those who have merged with the mainstream section of the region. On one extreme, one can think of those tribes located in places such as Andaman and Nicobar islands who accept their social, cultural and political independence as a matter of course and are therefore not involved in any self-conscious movements to assert solidarity. On the other extreme, one can think of tribals such as Bhumij of Purulia and Singhbhum who are too Hinduized to be effectively engaged in solidarity movements in the company of non-Hinduized tribes. In between the two extremes, one cannot think of movements such as the Naga National Movement and the Mizo National Front Movement launched by the Nagas and Mizos, respectively, and the Jharkhand Movement among the Chhotanagpur tribes who are involved in highly self-conscious movements for sociocultural, political and economic autonomy.

Looking at the tribal movements from the perspective of time, Sinha divides them into pre-British, pre-industrial and pre-market phases, early (1776–1857) and late (1858–1947) periods of British administration and finally the period since Independence (1947 and after).

In the first phase, there was what was called 'Hindu method of tribal absorption' (Bose 1941), by which is meant that the tribals were integrated in a slow but gradual way into the Aryan way of life without their cultural autonomy being compromised in a big way. This ensured that there were no strong tribal rebellions during this phase, although there was some resentment among some tribal groups (e.g. Bhils) about the low status assigned to them by the powerful encroaching Aryans (Navalakha 1959).

In the second phase, which is further divided into early (1776–1857) and later (1858–1947) periods of British administration, significant happenings took place. In the early phase, there was a growth in the volume of non-tribal immigration because of opening of new channels of communication and this led to an increased confrontation between tribals and immigrants. Tribes began to perceive economic, social and cultural threats from immigrants. As a result, there were a series of tribal revolts during the late eighteenth and nineteenth centuries (Sinha 2002, p. 256). In the later phase (1858–1947), in response to these tribal rebellions, the colonial administration put in place a number of legislative and administrative devices to protect the tribes from being exploited by the immigrants. This also helped them to follow their policy of divide and rule successfully. They constantly harped on the differences between Hindus and tribals. They sought to project Hindu religion and culture as backward and oppressive in contrast to the benevolent Christian (European) civilization. Europeans then appeared as a reference group for the new tribal elite. This schism between the so-called tribals and non-tribal Hindus was further accentuated by the creation of special tribe constituencies in terms of the India Act of 1935, which laid the historical basis for forming various tribal associations like the Jharkhand Party (Sen 1969, Vidyarthi 1969).

In the third phase (after Independence) emphasis shifted, in contrast to the British administration's main policy for tribals that aimed to consolidate tribal separatism along with limited welfare measures within its administrative framework. Independent India professed a policy of phased integration of tribes in the body politic of India along with massive welfare activities (Sinha 2002, p. 257). The most distinctive feature of tribal activities is that mostly they have been associated with the formation of new tribal political associations or parties. There has been an increased focus on the protection of their social, cultural and political autonomy.

It is possible to make some general propositions regarding the intensity of tribal solidarity and separate movements (Sinha 2002, p. 263). He says that the intensity will be positively correlated to an optimum convergence of factors such as ecological and social cultural isolation of the bulk of the tribal population vis-à-vis the core peasantry, location near the international and inter-civilizational frontier, a certain level of numerical strength and economy to provide the striking powers for solidarity movement, and a certain level of literacy and education to provide elite leadership. In contrast, if the above factors are weak, the tribal solidarity movements will also be weak or absent. For example, the Onge of the Andaman Islands are too isolated, have a relatively primitive economic base and lack of literacy and have not seen the involvement of literate elites. They have not engaged themselves in any intense tribal solidarity movements. They would simply like to see non-interference in their tribal affairs.

On the contrary, some sections of the Nagas could mobilize themselves strongly because their ecological isolation and location at an international frontier is combined with a fairly high level of literacy, a sizeable literate elite, and historical consciousness of armed conflict with the British and Indian administration.

T. K. Oommen looking critically at the tribal movements says that in India they have two main geographical and political anchorages (1990, p. 74). Movements among tribes of Central and Eastern India have been mainly oriented to their betterment within the Indian Union and movements among the tribes of the North-Eastern area have been essentially secessionist in orientation, which is reflective of their lack of faith in national framework and the very nation-state within which they find themselves. As Oommen says, the tribal movements in the former can be broadly divided into two types: those that emphasize the religious revivalist or reformist orientation and those that focus on the political separatist orientation.

One of the earlier attempts to study a large number of tribal movements was that of Stephen Fuchs (1965). He characterizes these movements as messianic or millennial movements led by rebellious prophets who are either individuals gifted with abilities to assume the role of a messiah or are allocated such a role by the community when it faces economic distress, social strain or political oppression. He suggests that the success of such a movement would depend on the individual ability of charismatic leaders. This perception, however, ignores the relevance of system characteristics in determining the origin and success of movements and the relationship between the types of leadership and social structure (Oommen 1990, p. 75).

Tracing the origin of different tribal movements, albeit in a brief way, Mahapatra (1972) refers to the religious movements such as Buddhism, Jainism in ancient India (p. 374), and Vaishnavism, which converted many groups such as the Meithei of Manipur, Bhumij of Bengal and Bathudi of Orissa. There were also many tribal uprisings when the British sought to expand its rule into tribal areas and stop raiding, feuding, head-hunting, human sacrifice or slavery in North-Eastern India and Orissa. He refers to the various tribal movements among Santhals, Oraons, and Mundas, which were inspired by Hindu priests or Christian missionaries. The influence of these people in these movements was clearly seen.

In Madhya Pradesh, there were movements among the Gonds inspired by charismatic leaders. Through these movements they claimed the status of the Kshatriyas and sought to purify the religious and social institutions in tune with the practices of high Hindu status. In Western India, often Hindu Sadhus or holy men have initiated religious and mobility movements among the Bhils (Fuchs 1965, p. 216). Significantly, he mentions that there is no prominent social movement, religious or political, among the numerically small, immigrating tribes like Biros' and Korwana. Second, there were movements for conversion to Christianity, which were inspired by the educated intelligentsia.

Rajendra Singh in his recent highly influential book *Social Movements, Old and New: A Post-modernist Critique* (2001) characterizes tribal movements as basically non-class, non-materialistic and non-revolutionary. He identifies certain salient features of tribal movements in India (pp. 252–254).

First, he says that they are characterized by two apparently opposite but actually complementary social forces of active participation and defencism. The former encourages the tribes to seek power at the national and local levels and strive for the benefits of modernization. In this way, they are inclusivist. The latter, on the other hand, express themselves in collective stirrings for the defence of culture, revival of dialect, script and style of social life, including the demand for semi-autonomy, non-interference and so on. They can be characterized as seclusionist identity-oriented tribal movements. Movements in the North-East and the Jharkhand region of India are examples.

Second, most of the tribal struggles were revolts against the State. Many studies show that the oppressive character of the British government led to various tribal uprisings (Arnold 1982, Guha 1989a, 1989b, Paul 1989, R. Guha 1983)

Third, the tribal movements are closer to the model of the 'old' classical movements because the essential issue is that of protection of their social, cultural and political autonomy. Although they contain some elements of 'new' social movements, they are not really new because they are not related to new social forces such as market economy, technology and communication.

Fourth, there has been peasantization of tribal communities because of the forces of development and modernization. The forest-based tribal economy has been transformed into a settled peasant economy of tribal groups. As a result, what has happened is that the tribal collectivities that used to mainly fight the State power and its institutional apparatus in the past have now started like peasantry to launch movements against local landholders. The emerging class conflict situation is seen as the outcome of the process of peasantization of tribal societies (Upadhyaya 1980).

Last, there has been growing consciousness among tribals to define their concepts of development and emphasize the need for autonomy and decide and regulate the flora and fauna of their region. One dominant tendency among tribes has been to try and gain access to power and privileges and not to deny themselves these things.

Although certain features can be identified that characterize different tribal movements in the country, and in fact there is a strong need for deploying a comparative perspective, one also needs to take a deeper and critical look at each of these movements. This would enable us to understand the distinctiveness of each movement.

It is with this purpose that we take a look at one of the most powerful and successful tribal movements, that is, the Jharkhand Movement.

K. S. Singh in a review of the tribal solidarity movements in Chhotanagpur, which later grew into the Jharkhand Movement, identifies the following reasons (2002, pp. 267–292). First, Chhotanagpur was the most advanced of the tribal regions as far as literacy, political consciousness and industrial development were concerned. Second, the major tribal communities were concentrated in a geographically distinct region. They were not scattered over different political and territorial regions. This provides a strong sense of identity. Third, the majority of tribal groups living in this region were under the strong influence of Christianity. The area became effectively evangelized. Christianity gave them a sense of identity. It gave them a history and a myth, accentuated the notion of private rights in land, promoted education and medical care and also emphasized among the converts a sense of separateness from the rest. Fourth, the Chhotanagpur tribes had a tradition of militant and organized struggles going back over a hundred years; struggles organized around land and not forests as elsewhere. Last, Chhotanagpur was exposed to the operation of many interests: the Bengalis formed a sizeable professional and land-owning community and the Muslims were a significant trading group. The Bengali–Bihari controversy over employment in the late 1930s and the Muslim League politics also affected the development of the tribal separatist movement.

One can also look at the different phases through which the movement has passed to appreciate its distinctiveness. In the first phase (starting at the turn of the present century), it was mainly the Christian missionaries and organizations that were involved in forging a sense of unity among the tribal groups (Mundas, Ito etc.).

They tried to motivate the tribes to overcome some of the habits such as drinking alcohol that blocked their development and took some welfare measures. The second phase (1920–1938) witnessed the growth of some organizations such as Chhotanagpur Improvement Society (Chhotanagpur Unnati Samaj), which sought to harp on issues such as employment for educated tribals, reservation in the services and legislative bodies and formation of a sub-state joined to Bengal or Orissa. While it tried to spread its activities to villages, it remained essentially an urban movement. In the third phase (1938–1947), the movement became radicalized with the birth of the Adivasi Mahasabha. This party became increasingly powerful as it sought to create pan-tribal sentiment and use that sentiment to demand not merely the formation of a sub-state but complete separation from Bihar. It received strong support from Bengalis who felt their interests would not be safe in Bihar and decided to stand by the tribals in their demand for a separate state. The Muslim League too supported this demand for a separate state because of their desire to form a corridor that would pass through the tribal areas and link East and West Pakistan. The fourth phase saw the rise of the Jharkhand Party, which called for the improvement of socioeconomic conditions of all the tribals living in the Jharkhand region, which included Chhotanagpur tribals as well.

It emerged as the major party in the Chhotanagpur Santal Pargana region and captured as many as five seats in Orissa also in the second General Election. However, its influence slowly came down due to the impact of development programmes on the tribals in the Chhotanagpur region, the split between the advanced Christians and relatively backward non-Christian tribals, the growing financial bankruptcy of the party and so on. This was reflected in the reduction of its seats in the Bihar Assembly following 1962 elections. The first phase (1963–1975) saw the movement becoming more radical in nature. This was possible because of the influence of the Naxalite movement, infiltration of extremist elements in tribal organization and entry of Leftist parties in the region. There was also a change of emphasis. It was from the demand for a separate state (it was not completely given up) to the issue of conditions of the tribals, the nature and consequences of exploitation, isolation and neglect. There is a better-articulated demand for a dominant role for the tribals in regional administration for better educational facilities and more employment opportunities. These developments have been conceptualized in terms of (a) fragmentation of the tribal party and factionalization of tribal politics, (b) rise of urban pressure groups and (c) political extremism, agrarian radicalism and cultural revivalism (Singh 2002, p. 275). Finally, the struggles launched by the tribals resulted in the birth of the Jharkhand State.

Tribal movements in the North-East India

The North-East India is predominantly inhabited by tribal communities. For example, 93 per cent of the population of Mizoram is designated as tribal. Some of the notable tribal communities in the North-East are Mizos, Khasis, Garos, Kuki, Bodos, Nagas and so on. Although they constitute not a significant percentage of tribal population in the country, in the states of North-East India they form a very huge percentage. The North-East India has seen some of the most powerful tribal/ethnic movements in the country. Therefore, any account of tribal movements in the country must give due importance to the tribal movements that have taken place in the North-East India.

Some useful attempts have been made to classify the tribal movements in the North-East India (Dubey 1982, p. 11). They are classified as follows:

1. Movements for religious and social reform such as the neo-Vaishnavite movement. This movement has had a great impact on the tribes of the Brahmaputra valley, the Imphal valley and on the hill tribes of Tripura, North Cachar and Miki Hills. Movements inspired by conversion to Christianity among tribes of Nagas, Mizos, Khasis, Garos also come under this category.
2. Movements for separate statehood with the Indian Union or more autonomy to the tribal areas may be included. Such

autonomy movements have been launched by the Mizo Union, the Garo National Council, All Peoples' Hill Leaders Conference, the Plain Tribal Council of Assam and so on.

3. Insurgent movements that took place in Naga Hills, Mizoram and a part of Manipur maybe included.
4. Last, movements for assertion of cultural rights may be included. Such movements were led by the Bodo Sahitya Sabha, the Tripura Upjat, Yurbe Samithi and a number of cultural organizations working in Arunachal Pradesh (Dubey 1982, p. 11).

Some of the specific factors responsible for the emergence of various tribal movements in the North-East India has been enumerated in many research works (Chaube 1973, Chaudhuri 1992, Datta 1993, Dommen 1967, Guha 1979, Sareen 1980, to mention only a few) and are listed as follows:

1. There has been a growing sense of tribal ethnic identity among the communities in the North-East India. Before the British occupied this part of India, most of the interaction among these communities was confined to families, clans and villages. There was an extremely primitive communication system. The impenetrable hills and forests proved a potent barrier in the process of inter-tribal interaction. There was no sense of a broader tribal ethnic identity because of the near absence of transport and communication facilities. This began to change under the impact of a number of sociopolitical and administrative factors. The gradual occupation of the land by the British and the efforts made by Christian Missionaries unwillingly began to impart a broader sense of tribal ethnic identity to them. This identity began to be used as a rallying point later on in the movements. The Mizo National Front movement in Mizoram is a relevant example.
2. The Second World War also made a huge impact. The area that was isolated to a great extent suddenly became the theatre of war where armies belonging to different parts of

the globe using sophisticated weapons fought each other. The physical, political and ideological isolation was broken. People got an opportunity to join the army and began to be exposed not only to the modern warfare but also to the political ideals of independence. They began to demand autonomy for themselves. By the middle of 1940s, a small educated middle class had emerged among the Nagas, Mizos, Khasis and the Garos, and they were interested in sharing the fruits of political power that was to be handed over to the elected representatives.

3. The policy of the colonial administration towards forests and land and increasing settlement of non-tribals in the administrative centres such as Agartala, Shillong, Tura, Lushai Hills (as Mizoram was then known as) strengthened their apprehension and led to the different forms of movements. In the post-Independence India, a sense of neglect was engendered by the unbalanced regional development contributing greatly to the emergence of movements. For example, the Mizo National Front movement that began in the 1960s was attributable to such a perception among Mizos (Nag 1993, Nunthara 1996, Ray 1982). Some steps taken by both the State and the Central government were also greatly responsible. The imposition of Assamese as the official language of the state (Mizoram, Nagaland and so on were districts in the state of Assam at that time), to give one instance, greatly accentuated their feeling of being socially, culturally, economically and politically isolated and suppressed.

4. Political elites in this part of India also began to nurture political ambitions and made instrumental use of the grievances and the sense of depression prevalent among the people of this region. Their efforts to gain access to greater political resources also resulted in agitations and movements. Events in the North-East India lend empirical evidence to the elite theory propounded by people like Paul Brass (1991).

5. The involvement of Western powers, Pakistan and China in encouraging insurgency and in giving shelter to their leader was also responsible to a great extent (Sareen 1980).

Interventions

Having examined the issues relating to development and the reasons for the emergence of various tribal movements in India, there is a need to explore what possible interventions can be made. Unless right interventions are made with utmost commitment and seriousness, the issues that we have mentioned above would continue to be escape attention. Some of the possible areas of intervention are as follows:

1. Deliberate and conscious efforts should be made to encourage the participation of tribals in the conceptualization, formulation and execution of development programmes. The very essence of these programmes would be lost if the tribals for whom these programmes are meant are not involved (Roy Burman 1972, p. 83). There is an urgent need for the institutionalization of their participation in tribal development programmes at different levels.
2. Existing political institutions such as district councils need to be politicized and radicalized. They need to be given more autonomy and powers to conceptualize, formulate and execute developmental programmes. Necessary funds should be allocated to ensure their financial independence.
3. Development programmes should be based on continuation of rights of communities over their local resources. Any attempt to snatch away their resources will be resisted as it happened in the case of a number of tribals, for example, the Mizos in Mizoram. In case of absolute necessity, one can think of an equalitarian arrangement whereby the resources are shared between the government and the local communities. For example, in Tura district (Assam) while bringing forest areas under reservation, the rights of the Nocte chiefs of

Namarang and Budwia as well as of the village communities have been fully recognized. The net revenue of the forests is divided in the ratio of 25:75 between the government and the chiefs and the villagers.

4. There has been an uncritical acceptance of shift of emphasis from jhum cultivation to settled agriculture. As many have commented, it is an impractical idea as the land is not conducive to settled agriculture, especially in the North-East (Roy Burman 1972, p. 83). Instead the emphasis should be more on scientific cultivation to reduce the adverse effects of jhum cultivation.

5. Great emphasis should be placed on the development of agro-based industries, training to improve traditional skills, supply of raw materials, purchase of surplus produce and so on. To generate employment opportunities, maximum emphasis should be laid on the establishment of small-scale industry.

6. There should be a comprehensive national policy on socioeconomic and cultural rehabilitation of displaced persons through an act of Parliament, which should include (Pathy 1998):

    a. All the alternative proposals must be explored before undertaking any large-scale project that displaces people and the opinion of all the persons concerned must be obtained.
    b. The cost of rehabilitation, environmental restoration and ecological sustainability of the region should form an integral part of the project.
    c. The Land Acquisition Act of 1984 should be amended to prohibit its misuse and define the term 'public purpose'.
    d. Regulation applicable to non-tribals for alienation of tribal lands be made applicable as far as possible to both public and private, national and multinational enterprises.

e. The quantum of compensation to be determined taking into account the value of the land and land-based survival resources.
f. Proper resettlement of oustees to ensure their socioeconomic and cultural survival with dignity in the hostile surroundings.

7. Education should be given top priority. The kind of education that is to be given to the tribals should be capable of equipping them with necessary skills so that their productivity is enhanced. Accent should be given on non-formal education so that they do not feel suffocated by the structure of formal system of education.
8. Appropriate steps should be taken to ensure that tribes are freed from exploitation by outsiders. The perception, real or imaginary, of being exploited by outsiders has been so acute among tribals that a number of movements have come up to free tribals from any outside exploitation. Although a number of protective measures have already been taken, one notices that they have not worked to a satisfactory level. Several factors like absence of official machinery, vast political influence wielded by the non-tribals coupled with indifferent attitude of the tribals and ignorance of existing protective legislation contributed to their ineffectiveness in practice (Pratap 1982, p. 292). Increased focus must be given to the removal of the above. One basic solution lies in involving tribal leaders at every stage of development programmes. Special programmes should be taken up to enhance awareness among tribals about tribal development programmes.

As the above account of tribal development would indicate, though it has been recognized as one of the most pressing issues confronting the democratic and liberal India, it has not been properly dealt with. As stated earlier, this is due to inadequate appreciation of basic issues concerning tribal development, a fact that would become evident from a number of tribal movements that have been taking place in

India. The North-East India is one such area where frustration and disillusionment among tribals has reached high levels. Considerable amount of unrest manifesting itself in insurgent and separatist movements can be noticed. Issues of deprivation, neglect and exploitation coupled with the very basic question of identity among tribals of the North-East India have become critical and need to be resolved at the earliest. It is in this context that the interventions we suggested be carried out would become important.

REFERENCES

Alam, J. 1989. Tribal identity in Jharkhand. In P. C. Chatterji (ed.), *Self-image, Identity and Nationality* (pp. 42–56). Shimla: Indian Institute of Advanced Study.

Arnold, D. 1982. Rebellious hillman: Gudem–Rampa Rising 1839–1924. In R. Guha (ed.), *Subaltern Studies I* (p. 110). Delhi: Oxford University Press.

Belshaw, C. S. 1972. Development: The contribution of anthropology. *International Social Science Journal*, 24(6), 41–65.

———. 1977. The contribution of anthropologist to development. In H. M. Mathur (ed.), *Anthropology in Development Process* (pp. 45–62). New Delhi: Vikas Publishing.

Bhattacharjee, S. R. 1989. *Tribal Insurgency in Tripura: A Study in the Exploration of Causes*. New Delhi: Inter-India.

Bose, A., Nongbri, T. & Kumar, N. (eds). 1990. *Tribal Demography and Development in North-Eastern India*. Delhi: B. R. Publishing.

Bose, N. K. 1941. The Hindu method of tribal absorption. *Science and Culture*, 7, 188–194.

Brass, P. 1991. *Ethnicity and Nationalism: Theory and Comparison*. New Delhi: Sage.

Chaube, S. C. 1973. *Hill Politics in North-East India*. New Delhi: Orient Longman.

Chaudhuri, B. (ed.). 1982. Introduction. In B. Chaudhuri (ed.), *Tribal Development in India* (pp. 17-37) New Delhi: Inter-India.

———. 1992. *Ethnopolitics and Identity Crisis*. Delhi: Inter-India.

Danda, A. K. 1973. *Tribal Economy and Their Transformation*. New Delhi: ICSSR.

Datta, P. S. 1993. *Autonomy Movements in Assam*. Delhi: Omsons.

Deniroff, R. 1974. *The Sociology of Dissent*. New York: Harcourt Brace.

Dommen, A. G. 1967. Separatist tendencies in Eastern India. *Asian Survey*, 7(10), 726–739.

Dubey, S. M. 1982. Inter-ethnic alliance, tribal movements and integration in North-East India. In K. S. Singh (ed.), *Tribal Movements in India* (Vol. 1, pp. 8–19). New Delhi: Manohar.

Dutta, L. 1985. Violence in India: The case of Naga National Movement. *Economic and Political Weekly*, 16(24), 1053–1055.

Duyker, E. 1987. *Tribal Guerrillas: The Santhals of West Bengal and the Naxalite Movement*. Delhi: Oxford University Press.

Fuchs, S. 1965. *Rebellions Prophets: A Study of Messianic Movements in Indian Religions*. Bombay: Asia Publishing House.

Gough, K. 1979. Indian peasant uprisings. In A. R. Desai (ed.), *Peasant Struggles in India* (pp. 85-126). Bombay: Oxford University Press.

Guha, A. 1979. Great nationalism, little nationalism and problem of integration: A tentative view. *Economic and Political Weekly*, 14(7–8), 455–478.

Guha, R. 1983. *Elementary Aspects of Peasant Insurgency in Colonial India*. Delhi: Oxford University Press.

———. 1989a. *The Unquiet Wood: Ecological Change and Peasant Resistance in Himalaya*. Delhi: Oxford University Press.

———. 1989b. Saboteurs in the forest: Colonialism and peasant resistance in the Indian Himalaya. In F. D. Colburn (ed.), *Everyday Forms of Peasant Resistance* (pp. 87-92). New York: M. E. Sharpe.

Hussain, M. 1987. Tribal movements for an autonomous state in Assam. *Economic and Political Weekly*, 32(3), 1329–1332.

Imchen, C. L. 1990. Issues in tribal development. In A. Bose, T. Nongbri & N. Kumar (eds), *Tribal Demography and Development in North-Eastern India* (pp. 40–46). Delhi: B. R. Publishing.

Karna, M. N. 1998. *Social Movements in North-East India*. New Delhi: Indus Publishing.

Mahapatra, L. K. 1972. Social movements among tribes of India. In K. S. Singh (ed.), *The Tribal Situation in India* (pp. 371–381). Shimla: Indian Institute of Advanced Study.

Nag, C. R. 1993. *Mizo Society in Transition*. New Delhi: Vikas Publishing.

Navalalkha, S. 1959. The authority structure among the Bhumij and the Hills: A study of historic causations. *The Eastern Anthropologist*, 13(1), 27–40.

Nunthara, C. 1996. *Mizoram: Society and Polity*. New Delhi: Indus Publishing.

Oommen, T. K. 1981. Social movements, national crisis and social change – the Indian situation. *NERC Bi-Annual Journal of Social Sciences*, 1, 1–17.

———. 1990. *Protest and Change: Studies in Social Movements*. New Delhi: Sage.

Pathy, J. 1998. Impact of development projects on tribals. In V. Joshi, *Tribal Situation in India: Issues in Development* (pp. 275–286). Jaipur: Rawat Publications

Paul, M. C. 1989. *Dimensions of Tribal Movements in India: A Study of Udayachal in Assam Valley*. New Delhi: Inter-India.

Pratap, D. R. 1982. Approach to tribal development. In B. Chaudhuri (ed.), *Tribal Development in India* (pp. 134-153). New Delhi: Inter-India.

Raghavaiah, V. 1979. Tribal revolts in chronological order 1778 to 1971. In A. R. Desai (ed.), *Peasant Struggles in India* (pp. 23–27). Bombay: Oxford University Press.

Rao, M. S. A. (ed.). 1979. *Social Movements in India (Vol. 1)*. New Delhi: Manohar.

Ray, A. 1982. *Mizoram: Dynamics of Change*. Calcutta: Pearl Publishers.

Rotter-Hogan, E. 1982. Insurrection or ostracism: A study of Santhal rebellion of 1855. *Contributions to Indian Sociology*, 16(1), 79–96.

Roy Burman, B. K. 1972. Integrated area approach to the problems of the hill tribes of North-East India. In K. S. Singh (ed.), *The Tribal Situation in India* (pp. 67–102). Shimla: Indian Institute of Advanced Study.

————. 1986. *Challenges of Development and Tribal Women in India*. Udaipur: M. L. V. Tribal Research and Training Institute.

Sareen, H. K. 1980. *Insurgency in North-East: A Study of Sino-American Role*. New Delhi: Sterling.

Sen, J. 1969. The Jharkhand Movement. *Seminar on the Tribal Situation in India*. Shimla: Indian Institute of Advanced Study.

Sengupta, N. 1980. Caste and tribals in Jharkhand. *Economic and Political Weekly*, 15(14), 664–671.

Sharma, K. L. 1986. *Caste, Class and Social Movements*. Jaipur: Rawat Publications.

Singh, K. S. 1977. From ethnicity to regionalism: A study of tribal politics and movements in Chotanagpur from 1900 to 1975. In S. C. Malik (ed.), *Dissent, Protest and Reform in Indian Civilization* (pp. 317–343). Shimla: Indian Institute of Advanced Study.

———. 1982. *Tribal Movements in India* (Vol. 1). New Delhi: Manohar.

———. (ed.). 1983a. Introduction. In K. S. Singh (ed.), *Tribal Movements in India* (Vol. 2, pp. 1-24). New Delhi: Manohar.

———. (ed.). 1983b. The tribal autonomy movements in Chhotanagpur. In K. S. Singh (ed.), *Tribal Movements in India* (Vol. 2, pp. 85-105). New Delhi: Manohar(85-105)

Singh, K. S. 2002. Tribal autonomy movements in Chhotanagpur. In G. Shah (ed.), *Social Movements and the State* (pp. 267–292). New Delhi: Sage.

Singh, R. 2001. *Social Movements, Old and New: A Post-Modernist Critique*. New Delhi: Sage.

Sinha, S. 2002. Tribal solidarity movements in India: A review. In G. Shah (ed.), *Social Movements and the State* (pp. 251–266). New Delhi: Sage.

Thakur, A. 2001. *Tribal Development and its Paradoxes*. New Delhi: Authors Press.

Upadhyaya, A. 1980. Class struggle in rural Maharashtra, India: Toward a new perspective. *Journal of Peasant Studies*, 7(2), 46–62.

Vidyarthi, L. P. 1969. Tribal situation in India: An appraisal of the leadership pattern among the tribes of Bihar. *Seminar on the Tribal Situation in India*. Shimla: Indian Institute of Advanced Study.

———. 1977. *The Tribal Culture of India*. Delhi: Concept Publishing.

———. 1981. *Tribal Development and Its Administration*. New Delhi: Concept Publishing.

Weiner, M. 1978. *Sons of the Soil: Migration and Ethnic Conflict in India*. Princeton, NJ: Princeton University Press.

10

Issues and challenges in tribal development

A perspective from the North-East India

Development has been a dominant category in social science literature for a while now. It acquired a preeminent status particularly from the 1950s and 1960s. The reasons for this pre-eminence are not hard to find. That was the time when many countries in Asia, Africa and Latin America became independent and began to confront poverty, illiteracy, ignorance and growing socioeconomic inequalities under self-governance. Earlier when they were under the colonial rule, the blame for their abominable socioeconomic conditions could be squarely placed on the colonial masters. Now that they became independent, they were expected to fend for themselves. This threw up challenges and possibilities. Massive expectations began to build up with the achievement of independence. Problems that have been part of their historical trajectory needed to be dealt with firmly and quickly. This was the context in which development became the panacea for all their problems. Development became the main instrument through which their problems could be dealt with and expectations and aspirations of the people could be realized. There was also another reason why it became a dominant idea. That was the time when the United States of America began to play a very proactive role. The ostensible purpose behind such a keen interest was to help the newly independent countries solve their long-standing problems and ensure minimum standards of life for their peoples. However, the real reason for this interest was to contain the spread of communism in the Third World countries. The USA was fully conscious of the fact that unless they were actively involved in the development programmes in the Third World countries, they would not be able to ensure that the influence of the then USSR was kept in check. Whatever may be the reason, the key point to be noted is that development became a dominant category. However, the *nature* and *character* of the developmental process that was sought to be initiated remained unproblematized. The logic of the development process was uncritically accepted. It was supposed to be free from all kinds of problematics. Any resistance to such a homogenizing and hegemonizing logic was viewed as retrogressive at best and anti-national at worst. Modernity began to be viewed as a kind of panacea (Kumar 2006, 2008).

Development and the North-East

The notion that modernity is a cure-all potion to be administered to get rid of inequality and arresting civic unrest accompanied the process of development in the North-East as well. Before we examine the kind of issues and challenges that the dominant developmental discourse threw up in the North-East, it would be in order to first have some familiarity with the North-East region.

The North-East consists of eight states. The eight states are Assam, Manipur, Tripura, Nagaland, Meghalaya, Arunachal Pradesh, Mizoram and Sikkim (which is the latest addition). The area covering the North-East is about 263,179 sq. km, which is nearly 8 per cent of the total geographical area of the country. Its total population is 38,857,769 and it accounts for a little over than 3 percent of India's population. The North-East has a density of 148 persons per sq. km. Arunachal Pradesh records the lowest density of population (13 per sq. km.) whereas Assam records the highest density of population (340 per sq. km.). (The above figures have been taken from the Basic Statistics of NER 2006.)

The North-East India is characterized by enormous diversity in terms of traditions, customs, ways of life, religions, levels of development, literacy rates, marriage patterns and so on. This diversity makes it highly problematical to consider North-East as a single cultural zone, as is popularly viewed. This is somewhat akin to the characterization of the South India as a single cultural entity. This writer has been asked many times whether he spoke Tamil and he has to reply in the negative as he is from Andhra Pradesh where Telugu is spoken. Similarly people from the North-East India too frequently face such questions. Not to speak of the North-East as whole, it is not unusual to find people of the same state (e.g. Nagaland) speaking different dialects. The point I wish to make at this juncture is that diversities of immense nature characterize the North-Eastern region.

There are some popular misconceptions that surround the North-East (Oommen 2008). One of them is that the entire North-Eastern region is dominated by the presence of tribal population. The fact of the matter is that only four out of eight states – Arunachal Pradesh, Meghalaya, Mizoram and Nagaland – are tribal-majority states and the remaining four – Assam, Manipur, Sikkim and Tripura – are populated mainly by the peasantry. Oommen would make a distinction between tribal and peasant societies. Peasant societies are part societies, whereas tribal societies are autonomous in nature (Oommen 2008, p. 5). We need to leave it at that for now and proceed to look at some other misconceptions about the North-East. Another popular misconception about North-East is that majority of the communities living here follow Christianity as a result of conversion over a long period of time. But facts speak otherwise. Only three out of eight states in the North-East are Christian-majority states and four are Hindu-majority states. For example, in Arunachal Pradesh 37 per cent of population follow Hinduism, which is numerically the biggest religious community. This diversion has been necessitated due to the continued prevalence of certain popular misconceptions that characterize the North-Eastern region.

As stated in the beginning, the hegemonic logic that was characteristic of developmental programmes that were implemented elsewhere also began to become part of the programmes implemented in the North-East. The cultural and structural specificity and needs and aspirations of the people living here have been ignored in the formulation of developmental policies and programmes in the North-East. One of the fundamental features of the North-East has been its landownership pattern, which is community oriented. The communal ownership of the land is under a serious threat because of the growing commercialization and privatization of land. According to this system of landownership, the land belongs to the clan/village as a whole but in a few cases it can be given to individuals for a limited period. According to the Report of the Land Reforms Commission for Khasi Hills constituted in 1974:

> The Commission is of the view that there are two main classes of land viz. (1) Ri Raid lands and (2) Ri Kynti lands under which there are many sub-classes known by the same or different names. Ri Raid lands are lands set apart from the community over which no persons have proprietary, heritable or transferable rights excepting the right of use and occupancy. Such rights revert to the community when a person ceases to occupy or use the land for a period of three year consecutively. Heritable and transferable rights over Ri Raid lands accrue when the occupant has made permanent improvements on the land. But even these rights lapse if he completely abandons the land over such a period as the Raid Durbar deems long enough. Ri Kynti lands are lands set apart from the time of the founding of the elaka for certain clans upon whom were bestowed the proprietary, heritable and transferable rights over such lands. (Report of the Land Reforms Commission 1974)

Communal ownership of the land is widely prevalent in other parts of the North-East as well.

One of the most important consequences of such a pattern of ownership is that it has not contributed to the growth of internal differentiation within the community, as there is no private ownership of the land. The possibility of the growth of socioeconomic inequalities has been dented. Because of the policy of isolation followed by the British rulers, this system remained unaffected during the British rule. However, after Independence, the ill-conceived policies and programmes of the government began to pose a serious threat to the pattern of the ownership of the land. It is being increasingly observed that the time-tested system of landownership is sabotaged posing a serious distortion in the land ownership pattern. The Report of the Land Reforms Commission for Khasi Hills (1974), for instance, has briefly mentioned some of the other distortions concerning the Ri Raid lands:

> The time-honoured system of administration of the Raid land by the village durbar is reported to be no longer observed. Indiscriminate issuing of pattas by the authorities has been a baneful cause of the loss of land to the real tillers of the soil. People from outside the village came to grab the land by means of pattas issued to them either by the village headman or the head or the Raid who may be influenced or otherwise won over to issue pattas to such people.

As stated above, what is observed in Meghalaya is also noticed elsewhere in the North-East. The policies and programmes have diluted the customary practices, causing immense hardships to the poor villagers. There is a growing tendency on the part of developmental agencies to be critical of the communal ownership. Instead of designing a strategy that could provide welfare without destroying such an egalitarian practice, they advocate a change from communal ownership to individual ownership both in agriculture and forest lands. The transfer of ownership from the community to the individual has certain serious implications. One of them is that the individual is not in a position to invest in the land as much as he is required to do thus reducing his chances of getting adequate returns from the land. He has come to depend heavily on the exploitative moneylenders and unfriendly government machinery, thus making one of the commentators to say that there has been a shift from 'primitive independence to complete dependence' (Karna 1990, p. 16). Furthermore, it has led to the intensification of socioeconomic inequalities that were not as sharp before as they are now (*Report on Development of Backward Hill Areas* 1981, p. 21). Without recognizing these issues, developmental programmes are being implemented. Although it has always been a stated objective of the government that any programme that is sought to be implemented in the North-East would take into account the institutional/cultural specificities of the area, what one notices today is that on the ground this is hardly the case. There is a wide gulf between proclamations and programmes. Unless this gap is seriously addressed, one cannot expect the developmental process to continue in a dialogic, harmonious and ecologically sustainable manner.

The dominant developmental discourse, apart from its emphasis on the transfer of ownership of land from community to individual, also puts enormous emphasis on the industrialization of the region, exploitation of mineral and forest resources over which the communities historically have had control and tapping of rich natural resources for sources of energy and power such as thermal, hydraulic or atomic. If this kind of developmental discourse is carried to its logical conclusion, it would involve certain consequences that need to be critically debated.

One of the dominant issues is that only certain strata or group of people have become the beneficiaries of development because they have been given the necessary assistance in terms of capital investment leading to the accentuation of socioeconomic inequalities in the region. This defeats the very purpose of developmental programmes, which are supposed to benefit people as a whole rather than any status group (Xaxa 1990, p. 28). A class of contractors, merchants, landlords and businessmen has consequently grown in the region over the past few years and their assets multiplied manifold. These people have developed a vested interest in current development discourse as they are free to invest in areas that yield quick and easy profits rather than those areas that do not, though they are important from the viewpoint of long-term development of the region, yield such easy profits. The growth of conspicuous consumption in the region can be attributed to the proclivities of this class of people.

Furthermore, because of the emphasis on production for market and profit, only commercial and plantation crops like potatoes, jute, coffee and tea, apart from horticulture, are encouraged, which means other crops are ignored. Liberal incentives are granted only for such crops that are commercially viable and yielding profits. As a consequence of the inexorable logic driving the current development process in the region, services like education and medicines have also been commodified and sold as paid services in the market, making them inaccessible for the low-income groups in the region's population..

The issues and challenges mentioned above are only suggestive in nature. Discussions here do not exhaustively address all the issues connected with the process of development in the North-East; however, these and other issues are engaging the attention of scholars, government functionaries and people in general. The issue of assertion of identity, for instance, which has given rise to a number of ethnic and separatist movements in the North-East, has been much commented upon and written about. What I have presented here so far is a brief treatment of the issues and challenges related to the development process in the North-East.

REFERENCES

Karna, M. N. 1990. Aspects of tribal development in North-Eastern India. In A. Bose et al., *Tribal Demography and Development in North-Eastern India* (pp. 7–23). Delhi: B. R. Publishing.

Kumar, D. V. 2006. *Modernisation and Ethnicity*. New Delhi: Mittal Publications.

———. 2008. Engaging with modernity: Need for a critical negotiation. *Sociological Bulletin*, 57(2), 240–254.

Oommen, T. K. 2008. Analysis of social change in North-East India: Some methodological issues. Keynote address delivered at the national seminar on *Social Change in North-East India: Processes and Responses*, 25 and 26 November 2008, North-Eastern Hill University, Shillong.

Report of the Land Reforms Commission for Khasi Hills, Government of Meghalaya, 1974.

Report on Development of Backward Hill Areas: National Committee on the Development of Backward Areas Planning Commission, Government of India, 1981.

Xaxa, V. 1990. Tribal development in North-East India: Trends and perspectives. In A. Bose et al., *Tribal Demography and Development in North-Eastern India* (pp. 25–30). Delhi: B. R. Publishing.

11

State and civil society

The context of Mizoram

Although the notion of civil society has always formed part of the liberal-democratic theory for quite some time, it has acquired a new salience and legitimacy in the recent past. The interest about the civil society did not originally arise because of any desire to study the civil society but because of the increasing disenchantment with the State (Beteille 2000, p. 173). The State in the then communist societies became enormously powerful and autocratic and in the West it has proven itself incapable of delivering the goods. In the former, the State sought to appropriate to itself various powers and functions, thus completely undermining the civil society. In the West and the Third World countries, the State promised a lot but delivered a little, underlining the need to look at alternative sites for development. The civil society presented itself as the only viable and meaningful site. People began to look at the civil society and the possibilities it offered. Faith was also placed in the market, but there has not been complete agreement among social theorists about the potential of the market to ensure welfare and development. Certainly in the recent past there has been a significant erosion of faith in the market. Market which was invested with so much power and faith suddenly finds itself in an unenviable position, unable to generate the same amount of confidence it once did, although for a brief period.

In India, too, the interest in civil society essentially arose as a result of disenchantment with the State (Kothari 1988). The transfer of power in 1947 unleashed enormous hopes and expectations among people. The State was expected to solve immense socioeconomic problems that had been existent for a long time. It was also expected to become responsive to the needs and aspirations of the people. It was soon realized that the State in the name of development began to throttle upon the democratic, socialist and secular order in innumerable ways. It began to serve the interests of dominant and hegemonic classes and whatever promises it made to the underprivileged and oppressed sections of society remained just that, promises. This created a great interest in the working of the civil society and emancipatory potential it was supposed to possess. It was expected to play a critical and instrumental role in creating a democratic and just social order.

State and civil society

Historically, the civil society has always been looked at as a sphere that is distinct from the State (as if they have nothing to do with each other) ignoring the important linkages between the two (Beteille 200). That would not be a meaningful way of looking at them. One needs to recognize the inseparable linkages between the two. For instance, the civil society needs to exercise a restraining influence on the State and prevent it from becoming autocratic and hegemonic and make the State fulfil its fundamental obligations of providing justice and satisfying the basic needs of people. In short, it is supposed to make the State do what it is supposed to do and not do what it is not supposed to do. At the same time, the State is expected to provide protection through its rule of law and administrative structures to the civil society organizations if they are threatened by vested interests and criminal elements. Not only that, it needs to tackle the structures of exploitation and oppression present within the civil society. For example, caste oppression, which is a structural feature of our society, needs to be sternly dealt with by the State.

The dialectical relationship that obtains between the State and the civil society needs to be placed in its proper perspective. The idea of civil society is based on the appreciation of the differentiation, not on the denial to the State of the powers and functions appropriate to it (Beteille 2000). Just as the State should not try to appropriate powers that do not legitimately belong to it, the civil society also should take care it is not overstepping its legitimate boundary.

Civil society: tracing its trajectory

The notion of civil society has had an interesting trajectory in the writings of philosophers. According to Hegel, for example, civil society is a sphere that exists between the family and the State. He locates the universal egoism of the civil society between the particular altruism of the family and the universal altruism of the State. For Marx, civil society is the site where private economic interests are advanced. Apart from making a few tentative statements, he did not write elaborately on the notion of civil society. It was Gramsci (1973) who provided valuable insights into the notion of civil society, though his conceptualization of the civil society does suffer from serious contradictions. According to him, civil society expresses, apart from economic interests, ideas, beliefs, values, customs and habits that have an impact on the State and the market. The contradiction arises from the fact that he emphasizes the historical destiny of the working class and the role of working-class party. Any conceptualization of civil society that singles out a political party as its pre-eminent institution is inherently flawed.

An equally serious note of the civil society could be found in the writings of the Scottish moral philosophers of the eighteenth century, most notably Adam Ferguson, whose book *Essay on the History of Civil Society* was published in 1767. The important thing to note about his work is that civil society and not the State is made the subject matter of study. Society consists of different but interrelated parts each of which contributes something to the working of the whole. For Scottish moral philosophers, the life of a nation depends not only on such grand institutions such as the State and the Church but equally on a multitude of ordinary, unnoticed and even obscure social habits and practices. Emile Durkheim, too, had a lot to contribute to the notion of civil society. He spoke of the decline of Church, the weakness of the family, the loss of communal ties and the underdevelopment of occupational and professional associations that shielded the individual from the State. The weakness of the civil society, situated between the individual and the State, is a general condition for political absolutism (see Turner 1994).

More recently, the use of civil society in exerting organized pressure on autocratic and unresponsive states and thereby supporting democratic stability and good governance has received critical attention (Hyden 1997, Mcllwaine 1998). The fact that civil social institutions can also be vehicles for participation in developmental programmes has also been noted (see Desai and Imrie 1998).

The Young Mizo Association (YMA) as a vital component of civil society

Having traced the trajectory, albeit briefly, the idea of civil society has gone through, we now proceed to examine the role of the Young Mizo Association (YMA hereafter) in the context of Mizoram. This would enable us to link the concept of civil society with the empirical reality that obtains in Mizoram. We look at the growth of YMA and the problematical relationship it has had with the State in Mizoram.

I developed an interest in understanding the nature and role of the YMA when I was working in Mizoram till some time back. I was interacting with people associated with the YMA and gathering valuable insights from discussions with them. This proved extremely useful in terms of locating the YMA and its role in the civil society.

In the context of the Mizo society, the YMA assumes an enormously important place. It is the biggest and the most powerful nongovernmental organization in Mizoram. It provides a classic instance of how civil society can make its presence felt through its well-organized associations. It provides an important link between the individual and the State in the context of the Mizo society. It is the organization through which the State tries to reach the individual and the individual the State.

The Young Lushei Association (as it was then called) came into existence on 15 June 1935. It was fashioned after the Young Welsh Association (Sangkima 1985). The association was the logical outcome of the process of weakening of Zawlbuk (Bachelor's dormitory) as an institution of great social importance in the Mizo society. The coming of the British, the advent of Christianity, the introduction of formal education and so on were some of the factors that were bound to significantly weaken the Zawlbuk as a social institution. The missionaries and some local elders were concerned that in the event of eventual disappearance of Zawlbuk there should be some other organization that should be able to channelize the creative energies of the youth of Mizoram. Thus was born the Young Lushei Association (the name was given by Rev. David Edward), a Presbyterian missionary. The YLA had three objectives to begin with (Sangkima 1985). They were:

1. To make the leisure profitable.
2. To seek progress for Mizoram.
3. To uphold and honour the Christian values.

In October 1948, the association was given a new name, Young Mizo Association. The constitution of the YLA, called Dan Bu, also elaborated on the ways to achieve the above objectives. The YLA will create an atmosphere in which members may utilize their leisure in a profitable way, which will lead to a healthy and proper life; the members will learn Christian ways of life, and the association would also organize games and sports, debates, discussions and dramas.

Because of the circumstances in which it was born, the YMA in its formative stage had strong links with the Church, particularly the Presbyterian Church, as the missionaries who were involved in the formation of the YMA were from that church. The strong linkage was reflected in the fact that to be an office-bearer of the YMA, one had to be a full church member. However, slowly the linkage between the church and the YMA became weak. This was also the time when the YMA developed a 'political' character. Due to the politically surcharged situation prevailing in the entire country, many members of the YMA could not really isolate themselves from the political movement for independence taking place elsewhere in the country. It did indulge in politically informed actions at times. For example, a serious encounter took place between the authorities and the YMA leaders when the YMA organized an informal meeting in 1945 in which McDonald, the superintendent, was also present. In this meeting the latter was informed in clear terms that the people wanted a democratic system in Mizoram.

Similarly, one of the movements of great political importance occurred when the YMA's Kulikawn (a locality in Aizawl, the capital of Mizoram) unit passed a resolution on the right of self-determination for the Lushais in April 1943 (Chatterjee 1994, p. 82). The Central Committee of the YMA, however, did not approve of the resolution on the plea that the YMA was not a political body.

In the General Conference held in March 1946, one of the agenda items was how to deal with 'Forest' (meaning the British). This angered the missionaries who left the meeting because the YMA was taking up issues on which 'it has no legitimate jurisdiction' (Sangkima 1985).

Yet another instance of incipient political consciousness among the YMA members was when they got an opportunity to send members to Burma with the ostensible purpose of spreading the Mizo language far and wide and doing good work to show that they sympathized with the people in Chin Hills, which were ethnically akin to Mizo. However, as R. Vanlawm, the then Secretary, felt the real motive was to promote the idea of 'Greater Mizoram' (Sangkima 1985).

However, at the height of autonomy movement in Mizoram, the YMA as an organization did not take any position directly, either supporting the movement or opposing the movement. Possibly because any such expression of position would have amounted to deviation from the original objectives that guided the formation of the YMA. The YMA being essentially a nonpolitical and social organization could not have taken such a direct political position.

As one former YMA leader said, the repressive measures taken by the Central Government could have also drastically affected even the normal activities of the YMA. In these circumstances, it would have been impossible for the YMA to take any direct political position.

However, one of the most momentous moments came when the YMA organized a huge 'peace procession' in 1975. The Central Government initially tried to ban it but relented later and allowed it to take place. The procession was aimed at drawing people's attention towards the excesses committed both by the Central forces and the underground MNF militants. It tried to expose the excesses committed by the paramilitary forces. At the same time, it tried to impress upon the people to resist the mindless violence committed by the MNF cadre. It left a positive impact on the minds of people.

The above instances of political activism can be accurately characterized as expressions of non-party political processes (Kothari 1989). The YMA, which is supposed to be a nonpolitical body, was becoming involved in the ongoing political processes in its own way. In fact, some of the YMA leaders were involved in political negotiations, and this fact shows that the YMA was playing a 'non-party political role'. In fact, as Rajini Kothari commented, non-party political processes provide sources of regeneration in Indian democracy. One can look at the role of YMA from that perspective. The above discussion is necessary to emphasize the fact that initiatives for non-party political processes are taken in the civil society as we have just seen.

What is, however, distinctive about the YMA is its social role, which makes it as the most important component of civil society in Mizoram and not the political involvement which was there but not sharply defined. It has been undertaking a number of activities aimed at enhancing the welfare of people. By successfully undertaking these activities, the YMA has shown that the civil society through its vibrant and forward-looking associations can achieve greater measure of success than the State with its indifferent and oppressive administrative structures.

During the formative years the YMA sought to make creative use of the energies of the youth by organizing debates, discussions, games and sports. Its role in encouraging people to maintain public health and sanitation has also been remarkable. It played a key role in establishing educational institutions. For example, the present Govt. Higher Secondary School (Aizawl) was established in 1944 with the active participation of the YMA. It has opened and is running a number of Adult Education Centres all over the state of Mizoram. It has played no mean role in making Mizoram the state with the highest (overtaking Kerala) rate of literacy in the country. When progress in the rest of the country in respect of increasing literacy is thoroughly unsatisfactory, it has been remarkable in the context of Mizoram mainly due to the efforts of the missionaries first and then the YMA. While one may explain the enthusiasm of the missionaries to make people literate in terms of religious motivations, one cannot find any extraneous motivation in the case of the YMA except the deep-rooted conviction that its existence can only be justified by making efforts to eradicate social evils such as illiteracy.

When Mautam (famine) occurred in 1959, there was a widespread disturbance in terms of unavailability of food (Kumar 2009). The YMA stepped in in response to a request by the Zoram Famine Relief Committee. The General Conference in 1959 appealed to all the branches to sacrifice all it could to bring some relief to the famine-stricken people. It received a positive response from the people. This was the time when the State deeply disappointed the people by not providing immediate relief. The YMA with all its limitations tried to do something that was really appreciated by people in general.

It plays an extremely important role in times of natural calamities such as landslides. It is not uncommon to see the YMA members reaching the place of accident much before the police do so and undertaking the rescue and relief work. The collective spirit that guides the work of the YMA is reflected in such circumstances and one's faith in the civil society institutions tends to get reinforced. As Emile Durkheim would have put it, it is an expression of the greater predominance of collective conscience over individual conscience.

Take the case of death. Death in a 'modern' society has become individualized. By this we mean that except for the most immediate family members or kin of the deceased, others are hardly involved in the rituals connected with death. However, in the context of the Mizo society, the death of a person is still treated as a collective loss. It seems as though the whole society is involved in mourning the deceased. YMA takes the lead in such situations. It handles activities connected with a death ritual (such as digging of graveyard, taking care of guests etc.) enabling the most immediate relatives to mourn the death of their beloved unhindered by mundane distractions.

More recently, the YMA has become involved in important activities such as wildlife and forest preservation. The State depends heavily on it in ensuring the above. For example, 'Green Mizoram Project' has been undertaken by the YMA since 1974. Some of the other activities in which the YMA is actively involved are controlling of crime, helping the poor in constructing houses, and organizing feasts during the time of elections where people connected with different political parties come and share the food, thus promoting cordial atmosphere among them. The activities mentioned above would give us a clear idea of what the YMA as a vital component of the civil society has been doing in Mizoram. In recognition of the services rendered by the YMA in different fields, it received a number of awards. For example, it received 'Indira Priyadarshini Vrikshamitra Award' in 1986 from the Government of India.

The essential strength of the YMA lies in the fact that it has been able to project a united and cohesive image. Members may belong to different churches, political parties and so on. However, when it comes to the question of engaging in the YMA work, they are one, and the overarching identity of the YMA swamps all other differences. This also explains the moral strength it continues to enjoy.

However, of late, what one notices about the YMA, as even some of the members closely associated with the organization admit, is that it has been trying to appropriate functions that legitimately belong to the State, thus contributing to tensions in the relationship between the civil society and the State in Mizoram. As one person associated with the YMA in the past as an important leader put it, the YMA is at 'crossroads'. When asked to spell out what exactly he meant by that, he said that the YMA seems to have lost its touch with the original objectives. It is now taking up many functions that its original objectives did not intend it to take up. There seems to be certain amount of confusion about the tasks it is supposed to perform. The assumption of new powers and functions has almost made it a parallel government. For example, as he put it, the YMA's involvement in the preparation of electoral rolls, acquiring gas connection and so on does not seem to accord well with its essential objective of rendering social service. These functions legitimately belong to the State. Denial of legitimate functions to the State tends to strain the relationship between the State and the civil society and blur the distinction between the two as it has been noticed in the context of Mizoram. The YMA has become such a hugely powerful body in the state that more often than not people are seen approaching the YMA rather than any government department for solving their problems. The bureaucracy with its usually nonchalant and unresponsive attitude discourages people from approaching it. Taking advantage of this situation, the YMA tries to put pressure on the government and usually succeeds in solving some of the problems of people, thus winning their confidence. While one does appreciate the YMA for coming to the rescue of the people, one is not comfortable with the real possibility of the distinction between the civil society and the State getting blurred.

Another source of criticism is that, as one YMA activist informed me, the YMA being a nongovernmental organization needs to maintain its critical distance with the government so that it can play its role effectively. However, this is becoming difficult because sometimes some office-bearers also happen to be government functionaries. Furthermore, the YMA tends to depend on the government for finance and other purposes. These things are making it difficult for the YMA to have a critical and creative engagement with the government.

Conclusion

As mentioned at the outset, the interest about the civil society arose as a result of people's disenchantment with the State. The State has completely supplanted the civil society in the communist societies and in the Western liberal democratic societies it has not performed whatever it has promised. Hopes then began to be pinned on the civil society, and popular initiatives for the welfare and development of people began to be made in the civil society.

The civil society consists of associations, organizations, clubs and so on. We have chosen to study one such association in the Mizo society, – the Young Mizo Association (YMA) – which has been playing an extremely important role in terms of ensuring the welfare of the people. It has been a great force in the Mizo society and occupies a significant part of the consciousness of Mizos.

The State and civil society need to respect each other. The State should encourage whenever meaningful and popular initiatives are taken in the civil society, and, at the same time, the existence of civil society should not be based on the denial of functions to the State. They need to take care that they do not transgress their legitimate boundaries. At the same time, the State needs to link itself with the civil society through various networks (Joseph 2002). In the context of Mizoram, the State can find an extremely useful network in the form of the Young Mizo Association. The interests of the people of Mizoram will be best served if the State and the YMA continue to work together.

REFERENCES

Beteille, A. 2000. *Antinomies of Society*. New Delhi: Oxford University Press.

Chatterjee, S. 1994. Autonomy movement in Mizoram: A historical analysis. In R. N. Prasad (ed.), *Autonomy Movements in Mizoram* (pp. 80–85). Delhi: Vikas Publishing.

Desai, V. & Imrie, R. 1998. The new managerialism in local governance: North-South dimensions. *Third World Quarterly*, 19(1), 635–650.

Ferguson, A. 1767. *An Essay on the History of Civil Society*. New Brunswick, NJ: Transaction Publishers.

Gramsci, A. 1973. *Selections from Prison Notebooks*. London: Lawrence and Wishart.

Hyden, G. 1997. Civil society, social capital and development: Dissection of a complex discourse. *Studies in Comparative Development*, 32(1), 3–30.

Joseph, S. 2002. Society vs. State. Civil society, political society and non-party political process in India. *Economic and Political Weekly*, 37(4), 299–305.

Kothari, R. 1988. *State against Democracy: Transformation and Survival*. Delhi: Ajanta Publishers.

———. 1989. The non-party political process. *Economic and Political Weekly*, 19(3), 216–224.

Kumar, D. V. 2009. Explaining Mizo ethnicity: The relevance of oppositional approach. *Man in India*, 89(1–2), 37–49.

Mcllwaine, C. 1998. Civil society and development geography. *Progress in Human Geography*, 22(3), 415–424.

Sangkima, I. 1985. Young Mizo Association: A study in historical perspective. *Proceedings of North-East India History Association*, Sixth Session, Agartala, Tripura, pp. 433–441.

Turner, B. A. 1994. *Orientalism, Post-modernism and Globalism*. London: Routledge.

Index